ALSO BY ANDREA LEE

*Russian Journal*

# SARAH PHILLIPS

# SARAH PHILLIPS

*Andrea Lee*

*Random House  New York*

Copyright © 1984 by Andrea Lee

All rights reserved under International and
Pan-American Copyright Conventions. Published in the United States by
Random House, Inc., New York, and simultaneously in Canada by
Random House of Canada Limited, Toronto.

Portions of this work have previously appeared in
*The New Yorker.*

Library of Congress Cataloging in Publication Data

Lee, Andrea, 1953–
Sarah Phillips.

I. Title.
PS3562.E324S2 1984    813'.54    84-43182
ISBN 0-394-53547-2

Manufactured in the United States of America
24689753
First Edition

To the memory of
Charles Sumner Lee

# Contents

# SARAH
# PHILLIPS

# In France

During the wet autumn of 1974 I heard a lot about another American girl who was living in Paris. Her name was Kate, and she was said to be from a rich family in Chicago—a word my French friends pronounced with relish, in a pidgin staccato. Kate was a photographer who specialized in making nudes look like vegetables; she lived on an immense allowance in an apartment near the Bois de Boulogne. She was an old friend of Henri, Alain, and Roger, the three young men with whom I lived, and in early October we tried several times to visit her, but each time a hostile male voice over the telephone told us she was busy, or out of town, or indisposed. Henri finally heard a rumor that she was being held prisoner in her apartment by her present lover and an ex-boyfriend, who were collecting her allowance and had bought a luxurious Fiat—the same model the Pope drove—with the profits.

The story was riveting enough when we discussed it over drinks at the Bill-Board, a nondescript café near the Rue de Rivoli, but none of my companions seemed especially concerned about Kate. Alain sighed and licked the ring of milk foam from his glass (he always ordered Ovomaltine); Roger thoughtfully rubbed his nose; and Henri, shaking his head at me in mock sorrow, said, "American girls!"

Kate came occasionally into my thoughts as I sat shivering and watching television in the big vulgar living room of Henri's uncle's apartment, where a penetrating chill rose from the marble floors. That fall I had only one pair of tights because my supply of travelers' checks was dwindling and I didn't want Henri to buy my clothes; over the tights, for warmth, I wore a pair of white tennis socks I'd bought in Lausanne in the summer. The socks, which I seldom washed, were getting tatty, brownish, and full of holes. I massaged my cold toes through my socks and tights and thought idly about Kate the Lake Forest debutante immured somewhere overlooking the rust-colored chestnuts in the Bois. She seemed to be a kind of sister or alter ego, although she was white and I was black, and back in the States I'd undergone a rush of belated social fury at girls like Kate, whose complacent faces had surrounded me in prep school and college. Idly I sympathized with her, guessing that she had a reason for investing in whatever thefts and embarrassments modern Paris could provide.

In October there was a French postal strike, which pleased me: I had painstakingly cut off communication with my family in Philadelphia, and I liked the idea of channels closing officially between America and France. The dollar was down that year, and it was harder than ever to live on nothing in Europe, but scores of Americans were still gamely struggling to cast off kin and convention in a foreign tongue, and I was among them. I had grown up in the hermetic world of the old-fashioned black bourgeoisie—a group largely unknown to other Americans, which has carried on with cautious pomp for years in eastern cities and suburbs, using its considerable funds to attempt poignant imitations of high society, acting with genuine gallantry in the struggle for civil rights, and finally producing a generation of children educated in newly integrated schools and impatient to escape the outworn rituals of their parents. The previous June I had graduated from Harvard, having just turned twenty-one. I was tall and lanky and light-skinned, quite pretty in a nervous sort of way; I came out of college equipped with an unfocused snobbery, vague literary aspirations, and a lively appetite for white boys. When before commencement my father died of a stroke, I found that my lifelong impulse to discard Philadelphia had turned into a loathing of everything that made up my past. And so, with a certain amazement at the ruthless ingenuity that replaced my grief, I left to study French literature in Lausanne, intending never to come back.

One weekend in Montreux I met Henri Durier, and at his

suggestion quit school and Switzerland to come live in the Paris apartment he shared with his uncle and his uncle's array of male companions and his own two friends from childhood, Alain and Roger. There I entered a world where life was aimless and sometimes bizarre—a mixture that suited my desire for amnesia. Henri was nineteen, a big blond who looked more Frisian than French. Though he wasn't terribly intelligent, there was something better than intelligence and older than his age in the way he faced the world, something forceful and hypnotic in his gray eyes, which often held the veiled, mean gaze of one for whom life has been a continual grievance. He was, in fact, an illegitimate child, raised outside Paris by his mother and adopted only recently by his rich uncle. This uncle held a comfortable post at the Ministry of Finance, and Henri, who had an apprentice job in the advertising department of Air France, lived and traveled lavishly on a collection of credit cards. When I met him, he had just returned from touring Texas, where he had bought a jaunty Confederate cap. Throughout our short romance we remained incomprehensible to each other, each of us clutching a private exotic vision in the various beds where we made love. *"Reine d'Afrique, petite Indienne,"* Henri would whisper, winding my hair into a long braid; he wanted me to wear red beaded threads in my ears, like women he'd seen in Brazil.

Henri's ideas about the United States had a nuttiness that outdid the spaghetti-western fantasies I'd found in other Frenchmen; for instance, he thought Nixon was the greatest President, Houston the most important city. I was annoyed and bored by his enthusiasm for chicken-fried steak and General Lee, and he was equally exasperated when I spoke of Georges Brassens or the Comtesse de Noailles. He couldn't begin to imagine the America I came from, nor did I know, or even try to find out, what it was like to grow up in Lorraine, in a provincial city, where at school the other boys gang up on you, pull down your pants, and smear you with black shoe polish because you have no father.

The apartment where we lived was in the Sixteenth Arrondissement; it was a sprawling place, designed with fixtures and details in an exuberant bad taste that suggested a motor inn in Tucson. A floor-to-ceiling wrought-iron grille divided the living room from the dining room, and the kitchen, hall toilet, and both bathrooms were papered in a garish turquoise Greek-key design. Otherwise it was a wonderful Parisian apartment: tall double windows, luminous wet skies, the melancholy soughing of traffic in the street below. When I arrived, the place held handsome antique wooden beds in each of the four bedrooms, and an assortment of boards and wooden boxes in the living room, dining room, and kitchen. Henri's uncle, who spent little time there, seemed indifferent to comfort, preferring to furnish his apartment with a changing assortment of male humanity. There was Enzo, a muscular young mechanic, and Enzo's friends, who were mainly Italian hoodlums; there was Carlos, a short Spanish Gypsy, who lived in a trailer out by Orly; there was a doddering Russian prince, and a wiry blue-eyed shadow in a leather jacket who Henri assured me was an IRA terrorist; there was an exquisitely dressed prefect of police, who sometimes lectured Henri, Alain, Roger, and me on *"la nécessité des rapports sains entre les sexes."* Manners within this motley company had assumed a peculiar formality: strangers nodded and spoke politely as they passed in the halls.

Alain and Roger both rented rooms in the Fifth Arrondissement, but they spent most nights with us, sleeping in whatever bed happened to be available. The two of them had grown up with Henri in the city of Nancy. Alain was twenty and slight-bodied, with girlish white skin and beetling dark brows. He came from a large and happy petit-bourgeois family, and although he tried hard to look as surly as Henri, he was generally amused rather than aggrieved, and a natural, naïve joy of life gleamed out of his tiny, crooked blue eyes. He loved to improve my French by teaching me nasty children's rhymes, and his imaginative rendering of my name, Sarah Phillips, in an exaggerated foreign accent made it sound vaguely Arabic. Roger, a student who sprang from the pettiest of petty nobility, had flat brown hair and a sallow, snub-nosed face. He was sarcastic and untrustworthy; his jokes were all about bosoms and bottoms; and of the three boys I liked him the least.

The four of us generally got along well. I was Henri's girl, but a few times, in the spirit of *Brüderschaft,* I spent nights with Alain and Roger. At breakfast we had familial squabbles over our bowls of watery instant coffee and sterilized milk (one of the amenities Henri's uncle had neglected was the installation of a refrigerator); late at night, when we'd come back bored and dreamy from dinner or the movies and the rain on the windows was beginning to sound like a series of insistent questions, we played a game called Galatea, in which I stood naked on a

wooden box and turned slowly to have my body appraised and
criticized. The three boys were funny and horny and only occasionally tiresome; they told me I was beautiful and showed me
off to their friends at cafés and discos and at the two Drugstores.

At that time, thank heavens, I hadn't seen or read *Jules and Jim,*
so I could play the queen without self-consciousness, thinking
—headily, guiltily, sentimentally—that I was doing something
the world had never seen before. Two weeks after I had come
to stay at the apartment, I returned from shopping to find the
big rooms filled with furniture: fat velvet chairs and couches
from Au Bon Marché, a glass-and-steel dining-room set, and
four enormous copies of Oriental rugs, thrown down recklessly
so that their edges overlapped to form one vast wrinkled sea of
colors. "They're for you, naturally," Henri told me when I
asked. "You were complaining about cold feet."

When Henri, Alain, and Roger weren't around, I loafed in the
apartment or rambled through the Louvre; the painting I liked
most was Poussin's "Paradis Terrestre," where a grand stasis
seems to weigh down the sunlit masses of foliage, and the tiny
figure of Eve, her face unscarred by recollection, looks delicate
and indolent.

If I was idle, all France around me was vibrating to the latest
invasion of Anglo-Saxon culture. The first McDonald's in Paris
had opened on the Champs-Elysées. The best French commer-
cials were those for Goldtea—artless takeoffs on *Gone with the
Wind,* with Senegalese extras toiling in replicas of American
cotton fields, flat-chested French belles in hoopskirts, and
French male actors trying subtly to inject a bit of Wild West into
the Confederate cavaliers they played. The hit song that fall was
a piece by the madly popular cartoon canary TiTi, who had
begun in the United States as Tweety; it was a lisping ditty in a
high sexy voice, and it seemed to be ringing faintly at all hours
through the streets of the city. French girls were wearing rust-
colored cavalier boots and skintight cigarette jeans that dug into
their crotches in imitation of Jane Birkin, the English movie star.
Birkin had the swayback and flat buttocks of a little girl, and she
spoke a squeaky, half-hysterical, English-accented French.
Henri, Alain, and Roger rolled on the floor in fits of insane
laughter whenever I imitated Jane Birkin. I had a pair of cigarette jeans, too; they left a mesh of welts on my belly and thighs.
Sometimes in the rainy afternoons when I walked in the Bois, I
could hear TiTi's song playing somewhere deep in the dripping

yellow leaves. Occasionally a wet leaf would come sailing out of
the woods and affix itself squarely to my cheek or forehead like
an airmail stamp, and I would think of all the letters I hadn't
written home.

In October we went to England three times, on weekend
excursions in Henri's plastic jeep. We took the ferry to Dover,
then drove up to London, where Roger thought it was fun to
play slot machines late at night in a penny arcade in Piccadilly
Circus. Each time, we put up at the Cadogan Hotel, charging a
suite to Henri's uncle's credit card. The respectable English and
Continental travelers eyed us surreptitiously, and we determined that if questioned we would say we were a rock-and-roll
band. "Josephine Baker et les Trois Bananes," suggested Alain.

Some chemistry of air, soil, and civilization filled me with
unwilling nostalgia, and I kept a sharp lookout in London for
certain types of tourists: prosperous black Americans, a little
overdressed and a bit uneasy in hotel lobbies, who could in-
stantly identify where I came from, and who might know my
family. During the day we would drive into the country and rent
horses, prodding them into clattering gallops with Comanche
yells. I was the official interpreter on these expeditions, and the
times when I failed to understand a broad country accent, the
three boys jeered at me. "What's the matter, don't you speak
English?" they'd say.

Later that fall we tried to take the ferry from Normandy to the
island of Jersey but were prevented from doing so by bad
weather. We spent the night in Granville, in a tall, chill stone
hotel where the shutters banged all night in a gale off the Channel. The next morning Alain got up, looking very skinny and
white in a pair of sagging blue underpants, and ran shivering to
the window. "We'll have to forget the island," he said, peering
through the shutters. The waves were slate-colored, huge, with
an oily roll to them and with shifting crests of yellowish foam.

Alain was in a bad mood because Henri and I had made love
the night before in the twin bed next to his. "That was a charm-
ing thing to do," he said to Henri, who was pulling on his jeans.
"To torture a poor adolescent. I couldn't get to sleep for
hours!"

He tossed a pillow at Henri, who batted it away. Henri and I
were in foul moods ourselves, mainly because the mutual fascination that had joined us suddenly and profoundly three

months before had begun to break down into boredom and suspicion.

Still in his underpants, Alain jumped up onto one of the beds and began to yodel and beat his chest like Tarzan. "Aaah!" he yelled, rolling his eyes maniacally; then he leaped upon Henri, who had bent to tie his sneaker.

"*Idiot! T'es dingue, toi!*" shouted Henri, and the two of them began to wrestle, Henri easily gaining the upper hand over the bony Alain. Alain groaned in pretended anguish when Henri sat on his chest; it was clear that this attack and defeat were part of a ritual whose rules had been set in childhood. They were far closer to each other, I thought, than I would ever be to either of them.

When Roger appeared, he was in as bad a mood as the rest of us, his back aching because he had had to spend the night on a cot in a tiny *chambre de bonne* two floors above ours. "What a room!" he said, grabbing my comb and stroking his flat brown hair still flatter. "Good for a midget or a paraplegic!"

We gave up on the island of Jersey and drove inland toward Paris, past fields that were bright green beneath October mists, and through spare Norman villages, and then past brown copses and woodlands, all under a sky where a single white channel was opening between two dark fronts of autumn storm. Raindrops broke and ran upward on the windshield of the jeep, and I shivered in Henri's aviator jacket, which he had bought in Texas. To keep warm we sang, though the number of songs all four of us knew the words to was small: "Auprès de Ma Blonde," "Chevalier de la Table Ronde," "Dixie," "Home on the Range," and endlessly, endlessly, John Denver. "Country roads, take me home!" Henri, Alain, and Roger would warble, throwing their heads back with a gusto that was only partly satirical: they thought Denver's music was the greatest thing America had exported since blue jeans.

In between songs we talked about Roger's sister Sabine, who was engaged in a battle with her parents because she wanted to marry a Jew. "Sabine is a fool," said Henri. "The thing for her to do is to leave home and do exactly as she pleases."

There was silence for a minute, as in the back seat Alain glanced at Roger. All of us had heard how Henri had left his small family—his pretty, weak-chinned mother and his grandmother, a meddlesome farmer's widow from Berry. The story

went that when Henri's rich uncle—whom the family discreetly
described as *"misogyne"*—visited Nancy he had taken a chaste
interest in the fifteen-year-old Henri and had given him twenty
minutes to decide whether to leave the town forever and come
to live in Paris. Henri claimed he had decided in five minutes and
had never looked back.

Alain looked out the plastic window of the jeep. "It's not like
that in my family," he said, his irregular face solemn for once.
"With us, attachments have an awful strength."

We stopped for lunch at the Cercle d'Or, a small inn near the
outskirts of Rouen. The place had a wood-burning oven, and we
ate lamb roasted over the coals, and goat cheese and Bosc pears,
and coupes napoléons, and then we drank coffee with Calvados.
By three-thirty in the afternoon, the semicircle of white-covered
tables near the fire was almost deserted and the restaurant
seemed hypnotically comfortable; padding waiters had begun to
set the places for supper. Outside, above a hill covered with
beeches, the rack of storm clouds had thinned into streaks of
blue, and a few rays of sun reached into the dining room.

A squabble had started between Alain and Henri when Alain,
for no reason at all, threw a mayonnaise-covered olive into
Henri's wine. The quarrel lasted through the coffee, when
Henri, to the amusement of the restaurant staff, ordered Alain
away from the table. Alain, swearing under his breath, shuffled
obediently off to the courtyard and lay down in the back of the
jeep; through the window by our table we could see his big
sneakered feet protruding from under the rear flap in an attitude
of careless defiance.

When he had gone, Henri said, *"Espèce de con!"* and Roger,
who worshipped Henri and was always jealous of Alain, allowed
a faint smile to cross his face. After that Henri stubbed out his
cigarette on a crust of bread and began needling me about my
appearance; short skirts were out of fashion, he said, and mine
made me look like a prostitute. "And wherever," he added, "did
you get the idea that you could wear a green shirt with blue
denim?"

"Americans don't pay attention to little things like the color
of their clothes," remarked Roger nastily, brushing a thread
from the sleeve of his immaculate tweed jacket. "Or the style of
their hair. Sarah, *ma vieille,* you're certainly pretty enough, but
why don't you put your hair up properly? Or cut it off? You have
the look of a savage!"

Henri giggled and grabbed my frizzy ponytail. "She *is* a savage!" he exclaimed, with the delighted air of a child making a discovery. "A savage from the shores of the Mississippi!" (He pronounced "Mississippi" with the accent on the last syllable.)

In the sunlight through the window, Henri looked very fair-haired and well fed. His round face, like that of a troublemaking cherub, was flushed with malicious energy; I could tell he was enormously pleased to be annoying me, and that he wouldn't let me off easily.

"I'm going to go see Alain," I said, and started to get up, but Henri held on to my hair and pulled me back.

"Don't go anywhere, darling," he said. "I want to tell Roger all about your elegant pedigree."

"Tell him about yours!" I said rashly, forgetting that Henri was illegitimate.

Roger gave a thin squawk of laughter, and Henri's face darkened. He picked up a spoon and began stirring the heaped butts in the ashtray. "Did you ever wonder, Roger, old boy," he said in a casual, intimate tone, "why our beautiful Sarah is such a mixture of races, why she has pale skin but hair that's as kinky as that of a Haitian? Well, I'll tell you. Her mother was an Irishwoman, and her father was a monkey."

Roger raised his hand to his mouth and made an indeterminate noise in his throat.

A small, wry smile hovered on Henri's lips. "Actually, it's a longer story. It's a very American tale. This *Irlandaise* was part redskin, and not only that but part Jew as well—some Americans are part Jew, aren't they? And one day this *Irlandaise* was walking through the jungle near New Orleans, when she was raped by a jazz musician as big and black as King Kong, with sexual equipment to match. And from this agreeable encounter was born our little Sarah, *notre Négresse pasteurisée*." He reached over and pinched my chin. "It's a true story, isn't it, Sarah?" He pinched harder. "Isn't it?"

"Let me alone!" I said, pulling my head away.

"That's enough, Henri," said Roger.

There was a short silence, in which Henri's eyes were fixed cheerfully and expectantly on mine, as if he were waiting for a reward.

I said, "I think that is the stupidest thing I have ever heard. I didn't know you could be so stupid."

He waved his hand languidly at me, and I shoved back my

chair and walked to the hall where the toilets were. All the staff had left the small dining room, which looked pretty and tranquil with the low fire and the tables freshly laid for dinner. The exception was the table where I had been sitting with Henri and Roger: the cloth, which hadn't been cleaned after the coffee, was extravagantly littered with ashes, wine stains, ends of bread, and fruit parings, as if filthy children had been playing there.

In the room labeled *Dames,* which was surprisingly modern—all red, with Florentine-gold faucets—I closed the toilet lid and sat down on it, bending double so that my cheek rested on my knees. It was a position to feel small in. I sat breathing soberly and carefully as I tried to control the blood pounding in my head.

I wasn't upset by the racism of what Henri had said. Nasty remarks about race and class were part of our special brand of humor, just as they had been in the wisecracking adolescent circles I had hung out with at school. On nights when we lay awake in bed, I often teased Henri into telling me nigger jokes, stories of the sexy, feckless little mulatto girl the French call Blanchette. His silly tall tale had done something far more drastic than wound me: it had somehow—perhaps in its unexpected extravagance—illuminated for me with blinding clarity the hopeless presumption of trying to discard my portion of America. The story of the mongrel Irishwoman and the gorilla jazzman had summed me up with weird accuracy, as an absurd political joke can sum up a regime, and I felt furious and betrayed by the intensity of nameless emotion it had called forth in me.

"Oh, dear," I said aloud in English, and, still bent double, I turned my head and gently bit myself on the knee. Then I stood up, brushed my hair, and left the bathroom, moving with caution.

In the vestibule I met the hostess, a stout woman with beautiful, deeply waved chestnut hair. She told me my friends were waiting in the courtyard, and paused to regard me with a shrewd, probing gaze. *"Excusez-moi, Mademoiselle, d'où êtes-vous?"*

*"Je suis des États-Unis, mais jusqu'à présent, j'habite à Paris."*

*"Ah, bon, les États-Unis—j'aurais dit Martinique. Vous parlez très bien le Français."*

*"Merci. Je suis de Philadelphie, pas loin de New York."*

*"Ah oui, j'ai vu des photos. J'ai un neveu à Montclair, dans le New Jersey. Mais vous, vous avez de la chance, habiter à Paris."*

*"Oui, j'ai beaucoup de chance."*

From an open doorway at the end of the corridor came the rich, dark smell of meat stocks and reductions; I could see into the kitchen, where a waiter in shirt-sleeves was spooning up soup at a table. Beside him, a peasant in a blue smock and with a red, furrowed face had just set down a big basket of muddy potatoes.

When I walked out to the jeep in the courtyard, I found that the day had cleared into a bright, chilly autumn afternoon. The clouds had blown southward, skeins of brown leaves rose in the wind and dissolved over the low wooded hills and the highway, and the slanting sunlight on the small gray village, with its thirteenth-century church, its lone orange-roofed café and gas station, had the mysterious empty quality one sees in some of Edward Hopper's paintings. It was the kind of light that made me think of loss.

Henri surprised me by getting out of the jeep to apologize. Apologies were hard for him, and he went about them badly, using his blunt sexuality, his natural tendency to domineer, and his adolescent harshness to turn "I'm sorry" into another form of bullying. "Don't sulk," he said, drawing his forefinger gently along my hairline, and I gave a sudden giggle. I could tell that he had been afraid not that he'd hurt me but that I would hurt his pride by withdrawing before he had finished with me.

By the time we'd reached Chantilly, it had gotten dark, and we were all feeling better. We had emptied a small flask of Scotch, we'd planned a sumptuous new outfit for me—cavalier boots, lavender stockings by Dim, and a ruffled black velvet dress—and Alain taught me a song that went:

> *Faire pipi*
> *sur le gazon*
> *pour embêter*
> *les papillons . . .*

After that, as the lights of the Paris suburbs flashed by, we sang more John Denver, yipping like coyotes at the end of every line. In between songs, Alain sucked on a tube of sweetened condensed milk, with a look of perfect infant bliss in his crooked blue eyes. When Henri told him to stop, that it was disgusting, Roger said, "It's no worse than your 'pasteurized Negress'!" and I laughed until I choked; all of us did.

Back in Paris, we went to Le Drugstore Saint-Germain to have
some of the fabulous hamburgers you eat with forks among all
the chrome and the long-legged, shiny girls. Poor Roger tried
to pick up two Dutch models in felt cloches (the film *Gatsby* had
just opened on the Champs-Elysées), but the models raised their
plucked eyebrows and made haughty retorts in Dutch, so that
Roger was driven to flirt with a group of fourteen-year-olds two
tables away, red-cheeked infant coquettes who pursed their lips
and widened their kohl-rimmed eyes and then dissolved into fits
of panicky laughter. In the record department of Le Drugstore,
we ran into Alain's friend Anny. Anny was a tall, sexy blonde,
a law student renowned for unbuttoning her blouse at the slight-
est opportunity at any social gathering to display her pretty
breasts. She couldn't open her shirt in the record department,
but she did take off her high-heeled black shoe to display a little
corn she had developed on a red-nailed middle toe, at which
Henri, Alain, and Roger stared with undisguised lust.

At eleven we went off to see *Il Était une Fois Dans l'Ouest,* and
watching the shootouts in the gold and ocher mock-western
landscape gave me a melancholy, confused feeling: it seemed
sad that I had spent years dreaming of Paris when all Paris
dreamed of cowboys. When we came out of the movie, the
inevitable rain had started up, and red and green reflections
from neon signs along the street lay wavering in puddles. Alain
wanted to stop in at a disco, but Henri was sleepy, so we drove
back to Neuilly, parked the jeep, and then dashed through the
rain to the big icy apartment.

It was much later—after Alain and Roger had rolled themselves up in blankets to sleep on the couches, and Henri and I
had gone off to bed to make love with the brisk inventiveness of
two people who have never felt much kindness toward each
other—that I awoke with a start from a horrid dream in which
I was conducting a monotonous struggle with an old woman
with a dreadful spidery strength in her arms; her skin was dark
and leathery, and she smelled like one of the old Philadelphia
churchwomen who used to babysit with me. I pushed back the
duvet and walked naked across the cold marble floor to the
window. Through the crack between the shutters I could see a
streetlight, and I could hear the noise of the rain, a rustling that
seemed intimate and restless, like the sound of a sleeper turning
over again and again under bedcovers.

Before that afternoon, how wonderfully simple it had seemed

to be ruthless, to cut off ties with the griefs, embarrassments, and constraints of a country, a family; what an awful joke it was to find, as I had found, that nothing could be dissolved or thrown away. I had hoped to join the ranks of dreaming expatriates for whom Paris can become a self-sufficient universe, but my life there had been no more than a slight hysteria, filled with the experimental naughtiness of children reacting against their training. It was clear, much as I did not want to know it, that my days in France had a number, that for me the bright, frank, endlessly beckoning horizon of the runaway had been, at some point, transformed into a complicated return.

I yawned and ran my hands up and down my body, pimpled with cold, feeling my usual absent-minded satisfaction in the length and suppleness of my limbs. Kate the photographer might make an interesting vegetable out of me, if I could only get to see her. Maybe tomorrow, I thought, I would go pound on her door; maybe her guardians would let me in. In a few minutes I darted back to bed and settled carefully onto the big flat pillow where Henri had his face turned to the wall. Before I slept, I said to myself, "I can stay here longer, but I have to leave by spring." And that, in fact, is the way things turned out.

# New African

On a hot Sunday morning in the summer of 1963, I was sitting restlessly with my mother, my brother Matthew, and my aunts Lily, Emma, and May in a central pew of the New African Baptist Church. It was mid-August, and the hum of the big electric fans at the back of the church was almost enough to muffle my father's voice from the pulpit; behind me I could hear Mrs. Gordon, a stout, feeble old woman who always complained of dizziness, remark sharply to her daughter that at the rate the air-conditioning fund was growing, it might as well be for the next century. Facing the congregation, my father—who was Reverend Phillips to the rest of the world—seemed hot himself; he mopped his brow with a handkerchief and drank several glasses of ice water from the heavy pitcher on the table by the pulpit. I looked at him critically. He's still reading the text, I thought. Then he'll do the sermon, then the baptism, and it will be an hour, maybe two.

I rubbed my chin and then idly began to snap the elastic band that held my red straw hat in place. What I would really like to do, I decided, would be to go home, put on my shorts, and climb up into the tree house I had set up the day before with Matthew. We'd nailed an old bushel basket up in the branches of the big maple that stretched above the sidewalk in front of the house; it made a sort of crow's nest where you could sit comfortably, except for a few splinters, and read, or peer through the dusty leaves at the cars that passed down the quiet suburban road. There was shade and wind and a feeling of high adventure up in the treetop, where the air seemed to vibrate with the dry rhythms of the cicadas; it was as different as possible from church, where the packed congregation sat in a near-visible miasma of emotion and cologne, and trolleys passing in the city street outside set the stained-glass windows rattling.

I slouched between Mama and Aunt Lily and felt myself going limp with lassitude and boredom, as if the heat had melted my bones; the only thing about me with any character seemed to be my firmly starched eyelet dress. Below the scalloped hem, my legs were skinny and wiry, the legs of a ten-year-old amazon, scarred from violent adventures with bicycles and skates. A fingernail tapped my wrist; it was Aunt Emma, reaching across Aunt Lily to press a piece of butterscotch into my hand. When I slipped the candy into my mouth, it tasted faintly of Arpège; my mother and her three sisters were monumental women, ample of bust and slim of ankle, with a weakness for elegant footwear and French perfume. As they leaned back and forth to exchange discreet tidbits of gossip, they fanned themselves and me with fans from the Byron J. Wiggins Funeral Parlor. The fans, which were fluttering throughout the church, bore a depiction of the Good Shepherd: a hollow-eyed blond Christ holding three fat pink-cheeked children. This Christ resembled the Christ who stood among apostles on the stained-glass windows of the church. Deacon Wiggins, a thoughtful man, had also provided New African with a few dozen fans bearing the picture of a black child praying, but I rarely saw those in use.

There was little that was new or very African about the New African Baptist Church. The original congregation had been formed in 1813 by three young men from Philadelphia's large community of free blacks, and before many generations had passed, it had become spiritual home to a collection of prosperous, conservative, generally light-skinned parishioners. The church was a gray Gothic structure, set on the corner of a run-down street in South Philadelphia a dozen blocks below Rittenhouse Square and a few blocks west of the spare, clannish Italian neighborhoods that produced Frankie Avalon and Frank Rizzo. At the turn of the century, the neighborhood had been a tidy collection of brick houses with scrubbed marble steps—the homes of a group of solid citizens whom Booker T. Washington,

in a centennial address to the church, described as "the ablest
Negro businessmen of our generation." Here my father had
grown up aspiring to preach to the congregation of New African
—an ambition encouraged by my grandmother Phillips, a formi-
dable churchwoman. Here, too, my mother and her sisters had
walked with linked arms to Sunday services, exchanging affected
little catchphrases of French and Latin they had learned at Girls'
High.

In the 1950s many of the parishioners, seized by the national
urge toward the suburbs, moved to newly integrated towns outside the city, leaving the streets around New African to fill with
bottles and papers and loungers. The big church stood suddenly
isolated. It had not been abandoned—on Sundays the front
steps overflowed with members who had driven in—but there
was a tentative feeling in the atmosphere of those Sunday mornings, as if through the muddle of social change, the future of
New African had become unclear. Matthew and I, suburban
children, felt a mixture of pride and animosity toward the
church. On the one hand, it was a marvelous private domain, a
richly decorated and infinitely suggestive playground where we
were petted by a congregation that adored our father; on the
other hand, it seemed a bit like a dreadful old relative in the city,
one who forced us into tedious visits and who linked us to a past
that came to seem embarrassingly primitive as we grew older.

I slid down in my seat, let my head roll back, and looked up
at the blue arches of the church ceiling. Lower than these, in
back of the altar, was an enormous gilded cross. Still lower, in
a semicircle near the pulpit, sat the choir, flanked by two tall
golden files of organ pipes, and below the choir was a somber
crescent of dark-suited deacons. In front, at the center of everything, his bald head gleaming under the lights, was Daddy. On
summer Sundays he wore white robes, and when he raised his
arms, the heavy material fell in curving folds like the ridged
petals of an Easter lily. Usually when I came through the crowd
to kiss him after the service, his cheek against my lips felt wet
and gravelly with sweat and a new growth of beard sprouted
since morning. Today, however, was a baptismal Sunday, and I
wouldn't have a chance to kiss him until he was freshly shaven
and cool from the shower he took after the ceremony. The
baptismal pool was in an alcove to the left of the altar; it had
mirrored walls and red velvet curtains, and above it, swaying on
a string, hung a stuffed white dove.

Daddy paused in the invocation and asked the congregation to pray. The choir began to sing softly:

> Blessed assurance,
> Jesus is mine!
> Oh what a foretaste
> Of glory divine!

In the middle of the hymn, I edged my head around my mother's cool, muscular arm (she swam every day of the summer) and peered at Matthew. He was sitting bolt upright holding a hymnal and a pencil, his long legs inside his navy-blue summer suit planted neatly in front of him, his freckled thirteen-year-old face that was so like my father's wearing not the demonic grin it bore when we played alone but a maddeningly composed, attentive expression. "Two hours!" I mouthed at him, and pulled back at a warning pressure from my mother. Then I joined in the singing, feeling disappointed: Matthew had returned me a glance of scorn. Just lately he had started acting very superior and tolerant about tedious Sunday mornings. A month before, he'd been baptized, marching up to the pool in a line of white-robed children as the congregation murmured happily about Reverend Phillips's son. Afterward Mrs. Pinkston, a tiny, yellow-skinned old woman with a blind left eye, had come up to me and given me a painful hug, whispering that she was praying night and day for the pastor's daughter to hear the call as well.

I bit my fingernails whenever I thought about baptism; the subject brought out a deep-rooted balkiness in me. Ever since I could remember, Matthew and I had made a game of dispelling the mysteries of worship with a gleeful secular eye: we knew how the bread and wine were prepared for Communion, and where Daddy bought his robes (Ekhardt Brothers, in North Philadelphia, makers also of robes for choirs, academicians, and judges). Yet there was an unassailable magic about an act as public and dramatic as baptism. I felt toward it the slightly exasperated awe a stagehand might feel on realizing that although he can identify with professional exactitude the minutest components of a show, there is still something indefinable in the power that makes it a cohesive whole. Though I could not have put it into words, I believed that the decision to make a frightening and embarrassing backward plunge into a pool of sanctified water

meant that one had received a summons to Christianity as unmistakable as the blare of an automobile horn. I believed this
with the same fervor with which, already, I believed in the power
of romance, especially in the miraculous efficacy of a lover's first
kiss. I had never been kissed by a lover, nor had I heard the call
to baptism.

For a Baptist minister and his wife, my father and mother were
unusually relaxed about religion; Matthew and I had never been
required to read the Bible, and my father's sermons had been
criticized by some older church members for omitting the word
"sin." Mama and Daddy never tried to push me toward baptism,
but a number of other people did. Often on holidays, when I had
retreated from the noise of the family dinner table and sat trying
to read in my favorite place (the window seat in Matthew's room,
with the curtains drawn to form a tent), Aunt Lily would come
and find me. Aunt Lily was the youngest of my mother's sisters,
a kindergarten teacher with the fatally overdeveloped air of
quaintness that is the infallible mark of an old maid. Aunt Lily
hoped and hoped again with various suitors, but even I knew she
would never find a husband. I respected her because she gave
me wonderful books of fairy tales, inscribed in her neat, loopy
hand; when she talked about religion, however, she assumed an
anxious, flirtatious air that made me cringe. "Well, Miss Sarah,
what are you scared of?" she would ask, tugging gently on one
of my braids and bringing her plump face so close to mine that
I could see her powder, which was, in accordance with the custom of fashionable colored ladies, several shades lighter than
her olive skin. "God isn't anyone to be afraid of!" she'd con-
tinue as I looked at her with my best deadpan expression. "He's
someone nice, just as nice as your daddy"—I had always suspected Aunt Lily of having a crush on my father—"and he loves
you, in the same way your daddy does!"

"You would make us all so happy!" I was told at different
times by Aunt Lily, Aunt Emma, and Aunt May. The only people
who said nothing at all were Mama and Daddy, but I sensed in
them a thoughtful, suppressed wistfulness that maddened me.

After the hymn, Daddy read aloud a few verses from the third
chapter of Luke, verses I recognized in the almost instinctive
way in which I was familiar with all of the well-traveled parts of
the Old and New Testaments. "Prepare the way of the Lord,
make his paths straight," read my father in a mild voice. "Every

valley shall be filled, and every mountain and hill shall be brought low, and the crooked shall be made straight, and the rough paths made smooth, and all flesh shall see the salvation of God."

He had a habit of pausing to fix his gaze on part of the congregation as he read, and that Sunday he seemed to be talking to a small group of strangers who sat in the front row. These visitors were young white men and women, students from Philadelphia colleges, who for the past year had been coming to hear him talk. It was hard to tell them apart: all the men seemed to have beards, and the women wore their hair long and straight. Their informal clothes stood out in that elaborate assembly, and church members whispered angrily that the young women didn't wear hats. I found the students appealing and rather romantic, with their earnest eyes and timid air of being perpetually sorry about something. It was clear that they had good intentions, and I couldn't understand why so many of the adults in the congregation seemed to dislike them so much. After services, they would hover around Daddy. "Never a more beautiful civil rights sermon!" they would say in low, fervent voices. Sometimes they seemed to have tears in their eyes.

I wasn't impressed by their praise of my father; it was only what everyone said. People called him a champion of civil rights; he gave speeches on the radio, and occasionally he appeared on television. (The first time I'd seen him on Channel 5, I'd been gravely disappointed by the way he looked: the bright lights exaggerated the furrows that ran between his nose and mouth, and his narrow eyes gave him a sinister air; he looked like an Oriental villain in a Saturday afternoon thriller.) During the past year he had organized a boycott that integrated the staff of a huge frozen-food plant in Philadelphia, and he'd been away several times to attend marches and meetings in the South. I was privately embarrassed to have a parent who freely admitted going to jail in Alabama, but the students who visited New African seemed to think it almost miraculous. Their conversations with my father were peppered with references to places I had never seen, towns I imagined as being swathed in a mist of darkness visible: Selma, Macon, Birmingham, Biloxi.

Matthew and I had long ago observed that what Daddy generally did in his sermons was to speak very softly and then surprise everyone with a shout. Of course, I knew that there was more

to it than that; even in those days I recognized a genius of
personality in my father. He loved crowds, handling them with
the expert good humor of a man entirely in his element. At
church banquets, at the vast annual picnic that was held beside
a lake in New Jersey, or at any gathering in the backyards and
living rooms of the town where we lived, the sound I heard most
often was the booming of my father's voice followed by shouts
of laughter from the people around him. He had a passion for
oratory; at home, he infuriated Matthew and me by staging
absurd debates at the dinner table, verbal melees that he won
quite selfishly, with a loud crow of delight at his own virtuosity.
"Is a fruit a vegetable?" he would demand. "Is a zipper a machine?" Matthew and I would plead with him to be quiet as we
strained to get our own points across, but it was no use. When
the last word had resounded and we sat looking at him in irritated silence, he would clear his throat, settle his collar, and
resume eating, his face still glowing with an irrepressible glee.

When he preached, he showed the same private delight. A
look of rapt pleasure seemed to broaden and brighten the contours of his angular face until it actually appeared to give off
light as he spoke. He could preach in two very different ways.
One was the delicate, sonorous idiom of formal oratory, with
which he must have won the prizes he held from his seminary
days. The second was a hectoring, insinuating, incantatory tone,
full of the rhythms of the South he had never lived in, linking
him to generations of thunderous Baptist preachers. When he
used this tone, as he was doing now, affectionate laughter rip-
pled through the pews.

"I know," he said, looking out over the congregation and
blinking his eyes rapidly, "that there are certain people in this
room—oh, I don't have to name names or point a finger—who
have ignored that small true voice, the voice that is the voice of
Jesus calling out in the shadowy depths of the soul. And while
you all are looking around and wondering just who those 'certain people' are, I want to tell you all a secret: they are you and
me, and your brother-in-law, and every man, woman, and child
in this room this morning. All of us listen to our bellies when
they tell us it is time to eat, we pay attention to our eyes when
they grow heavy from wanting sleep, but when it comes to the
sacred knowledge our hearts can offer, we are deaf, dumb, blind,
and senseless. Throw away that blindness, that deafness, that
sulky indifference. When all the world lies to you, Jesus will tell

you what is right. Listen to him. Call on him. In these times of confusion, when there are a dozen different ways to turn, and Mama and Papa can't help you, trust Jesus to set you straight. Listen to him. The Son of God has the answers. Call on him. Call on him. Call on him."

The sermon was punctuated with an occasional loud "Amen!" from Miss Middleton, an excitable old lady whose eyes flashed defiantly at the reproving faces of those around her. New African was not the kind of Baptist church where shouting was a normal part of the service; I occasionally heard my father mock the staid congregation by calling it Saint African. Whenever Miss Middleton loosed her tongue (sometimes she went off into fits of rapturous shrieks and had to be helped out of the service by the church nurse), my mother and aunts exchanged grimaces and shrugged, as if confronted by incomprehensibly barbarous behavior.

When Daddy had spoken the final words of the sermon, he drank a glass of water and vanished through a set of red velvet curtains to the right of the altar. At the same time, the choir began to sing what was described in the church bulletin as a "selection." These selections were always arenas for the running dispute between the choirmaster and the choir. Jordan Grimes, the choirmaster, was a Curtis graduate who was partial to Handel, but the choir preferred artistic spirituals performed in the lush, heroic style of Paul Robeson. Grimes had triumphed that Sunday. As the choir gave a spirited but unwilling rendition of Agnus Dei, I watched old Deacon West smile in approval. A Spanish-American War veteran, he admitted to being ninety-four but was said to be older; his round yellowish face, otherwise unwrinkled, bore three deep, deliberate-looking horizontal creases on the brow, like carvings on a scarab. "That old man is as flirtatious as a boy of twenty!" my mother often said, watching his stiff, courtly movements among the ladies of the church. Sometimes he gave me a dry kiss and a piece of peppermint candy after the service; I liked his crackling white collars and smell of bay rum.

The selection ended; Jordan Grimes struck two deep chords on the organ, and the lights in the church went low. A subtle stir ran through the congregation, and I moved closer to my mother. This was the moment that fascinated and disturbed me more than anything else at church: the prelude to the ceremony of baptism. Deacon West rose and drew open the draperies that

had been closed around the baptismal pool, and there stood my
father in water to his waist. The choir began to sing:

> We're marching to Zion,
> Beautiful, beautiful Zion,
> We're marching upward to Zion,
> The beautiful city of God!

Down the aisle, guided by two church mothers, came a procession of eight children and adolescents. They wore white robes,
the girls with white ribbons in their hair, and they all had solemn
expressions of terror on their faces. I knew each one of them.
There was Billy Price, a big, slow-moving boy of thirteen, the
son of Deacon Price. There were the Duckery twins. There was
Caroline Piggee, whom I hated because of her long, soft black
curls, her dimpled pink face, and her lisp that ravished grownups. There was Georgie Battis and Sue Anne Ivory, and Wendell
and Mabel Cullen.

My mother gave me a nudge. "Run up to the side of the pool!"
she whispered. It was the custom for unbaptized children to
watch the ceremony from the front of the church. They sat on
the knees of the deacons and church mothers, and it was not
unusual for a child to volunteer then and there for next month's
baptism. I made my way quickly down the dark aisle, feeling the
carpet slip under the smooth soles of my patent-leather shoes.

When I reached the side of the pool, I sat down in the bony
lap of Bessie Gray, an old woman who often took care of Matthew and me when our parents were away; we called her Aunt
Bessie. She was a fanatically devout Christian whose strict ideas
on child-rearing had evolved over decades of domestic service
to a rich white family in Delaware. The link between us, a mixture of hostility and grudging affection, had been forged in
hours of pitched battles over bedtimes and proper behavior.
Her worshipful respect for my father, whom she called "the
Rev," was exceeded only by her pride—the malice-tinged pride
of an omniscient family servant—in her "white children," to
whom she often unflatteringly compared Matthew and me. It
was easy to see why my mother and her circle of fashionable
matrons described Bessie Gray as "archaic"—one had only to
look at her black straw hat attached with three enormous old-
fashioned pins to her knot of frizzy white hair. Her lean, brown-
skinned face was dominated by a hawk nose inherited from some

Indian ancestor and punctuated by a big black mole; her eyes were small, shrewd, and baleful. She talked in ways that were already passing into history and parody, and she wore a thick orange face powder that smelled like dead leaves.

I leaned against her spare bosom and watched the other children clustered near the pool, their bonnets and hair ribbons and round heads outlined in the dim light. For a minute it was very still. Somewhere in the hot, darkened church a baby gave a fretful murmur; from outside came the sound of cars passing in the street. The candidates for baptism, looking stiff and self-conscious, stood lined up on the short stairway leading to the pool. Sue Anne Ivory fiddled with her sleeve and then put her fingers in her mouth.

Daddy spoke the opening phrases of the ceremony: "In the Baptist Church, we do not baptize infants, but believe that a person must choose salvation for himself."

I didn't listen to the words; what I noticed was the music of the whole—how the big voice darkened and lightened in tone, and how the grand architecture of the Biblical sentences ennobled the voice. The story, of course, was about Jesus and John the Baptist. One phrase struck me newly each time: "This is my beloved son, in whom I am well pleased!" Daddy sang out these words in a clear, triumphant tone, and the choir echoed him. Ever since I could understand it, this phrase had made me feel melancholy; it seemed to expose a hard knot of disobedience that had always lain inside me. When I heard it, I thought enviously of Matthew, for whom life seemed to be a sedate and ordered affair: he, not I, was a child in whom a father could be well pleased.

Daddy beckoned to Billy Price, the first baptismal candidate in line, and Billy, ungainly in his white robe, descended the steps into the pool. In soft, slow voices the choir began to sing:

> Wade in the water,
> Wade in the water, children,
> Wade in the water,
> God gonna trouble
> The water.

In spite of Jordan Grimes's efforts, the choir swayed like a gospel chorus as it sang this spiritual; the result was to add an eerie jazz beat to the minor chords. The music gave me goose-

flesh. Daddy had told me that this was the same song that the
slaves had sung long ago in the South, when they gathered to
be baptized in rivers and streams. Although I cared little about
history, and found it hard to picture the slaves as being any
ancestors of mine, I could clearly imagine them coming together
beside a broad muddy river that wound away between trees
drooping with strange vegetation. They walked silently in lines,
their faces very black against their white clothes, leading their
children. The whole scene was bathed in the heavy golden light
that meant age and solemnity, the same light that seemed to
weigh down the Israelites in illustrated volumes of Bible stories,
and that shone now from the baptismal pool, giving the ceremony the air of a spectacle staged in a dream.

All attention in the darkened auditorium was now focused on
the pool, where between the red curtains my father stood holding Billy Price by the shoulders. Daddy stared into Billy's face,
and the boy stared back, his lips set and trembling. "And now,
by the power invested in me," said Daddy, "I baptize you in the
name of the Father, the Son, and the Holy Ghost." As he pronounced these words, he conveyed a tenderness as efficient and
impersonal as a physician's professional manner; beneath it,
however, I could see a strong private gladness, the same delight
that transformed his face when he preached a sermon. He
paused to flick a drop of water off his forehead, and then, with
a single smooth, powerful motion of his arms, he laid Billy Price
back into the water as if he were putting an infant to bed. I
caught my breath as the boy went backward. When he came up,
sputtering, two church mothers helped him out of the pool and
through a doorway into a room where he would be dried and
dressed. Daddy shook the water from his hands and gave a slight
smile as another child entered the pool.

One by one, the baptismal candidates descended the steps.
Sue Anne Ivory began to cry and had to be comforted. Caroline
Piggee blushed and looked up at my father with such a coquett-
ish air that I jealously wondered how he could stand it. After a
few baptisms my attention wandered, and I began to gnaw the
edge of my thumb and to peer at the pale faces of the visiting
college students. Then I thought about Matthew, who had
punched me in the arm that morning and had shouted, "No
punchbacks!" I thought as well about a collection of horse chestnuts I meant to assemble in the fall, and about two books, one
whose subject was adults and divorces, and another, by E. Nes-

bit, that continued the adventures of the Bastable children.

After Wendell Cullen had left the water (glancing uneasily back at the wet robe trailing behind him), Daddy stood alone among the curtains and the mirrors. The moving reflections from the pool made the stuffed dove hanging over him seem to flutter on its string. "Dear Lord," said Daddy, as Jordan Grimes struck a chord, "bless these children who have chosen to be baptized in accordance with your teaching, and who have been reborn to carry out your work. In each of them, surely, you are well pleased." He paused, staring out into the darkened auditorium. "And if there is anyone out there—man, woman, child—who wishes to be baptized next month, let him come forward now." He glanced around eagerly. "Oh, do come forward and give Christ your heart and give me your hand!"

Just then Aunt Bessie gave me a little shake and whispered sharply, "Go on up and accept Jesus!"

I stiffened and dug my bitten fingernails into my palms. The last clash of wills I had had with Aunt Bessie had been when she, crazily set in her old southern attitudes, had tried to make me wear an enormous straw hat, as her "white children" did, when I played outside in the sun. The old woman had driven me to madness, and I had ended up spanked and sullen, crouching moodily under the dining-room table. But this was different, outrageous, none of her business, I thought. I shook my head violently and she took advantage of the darkness in the church to seize both of my shoulders and jounce me with considerable roughness, whispering, "Now, listen, young lady! Your daddy up there is calling you to Christ. Your big brother has already offered his soul to the Lord. Now Daddy wants his little girl to step forward."

"No, he doesn't." I glanced at the baptismal pool, where my father was clasping the hand of a strange man who had come up to him. I hoped that this would distract Aunt Bessie, but she was tireless.

"Your mama and your aunt Lily and your aunt May all want you to answer the call. You're hurting them when you say no to Jesus."

"No, I'm not!" I spoke out loud and I saw the people nearby turn to look at me. At the sound of my voice, Daddy, who was a few yards away, faltered for a minute in what he was saying and glanced over in my direction.

Aunt Bessie seemed to lose her head. She stood up abruptly,

pulling me with her, and, while I was still frozen in a dreadful
paralysis, tried to drag me down the aisle toward my father. The
two of us began a brief struggle that could not have lasted for
more than a few seconds but that seemed an endless mortal
conflict—my slippery patent-leather shoes braced against the
floor, my straw hat sliding cockeyed and lodging against one ear,
my right arm twisting and twisting in the iron circle of the old
woman's grip, my nostrils full of the dead-leaf smell of her
powder and black skirts. In an instant I had wrenched my arm
free and darted up the aisle toward Mama, my aunts, and Matthew. As I slipped past the pews in the darkness, I imagined that
I could feel eyes fixed on me and hear whispers. "What'd you
do, dummy?" whispered Matthew, tugging on my sash as I
reached our pew, but I pushed past him without answering.
Although it was hot in the church, my teeth were chattering: it
was the first time I had won a battle with a grownup, and the
earth seemed to be about to cave in beneath me. I squeezed in
between Mama and Aunt Lily just as the lights came back on in
the church. In the baptismal pool, Daddy raised his arms for the
last time. "The Lord bless you and keep you," came his big
voice. "The Lord be gracious unto you, and give you peace."

What was curious was how uncannily subdued my parents
were when they heard of my skirmish with Aunt Bessie. Normally they were swift to punish Matthew and me for misbehavior
in church and for breaches in politeness toward adults; this
episode combined the two, and smacked of sacrilege besides.
Yet once I had made an unwilling apology to the old woman (as
I kissed her she shot me such a vengeful glare that I realized that
forever after it was to be war to the death between the two of
us), I was permitted, once we had driven home, to climb up into
the green shade of the big maple tree I had dreamed of throughout the service. In those days, more than now, I fell away into
a remote dimension whenever I opened a book; that afternoon,
as I sat with rings of sunlight and shadow moving over my arms
and legs, and winged yellow seeds plopping down on the pages
of *The Story of the Treasure Seekers,* I felt a vague uneasiness float-
ing in the back of my mind—a sense of having misplaced something, of being myself misplaced. I was holding myself quite
aloof from considering what had happened, as I did with most
serious events, but through the adventures of the Bastables I
kept remembering the way my father had looked when he'd
heard what had happened. He hadn't looked severe or angry,

but merely puzzled, and he had regarded me with the same puzzled expression, as if he'd just discovered that I existed and didn't know what to do with me. "What happened, Sairy?" he asked, using an old baby nickname, and I said, "I didn't want to go up there." I hadn't cried at all, and that was another curious thing.

After that Sunday, through some adjustment in the adult spheres beyond my perception, all pressure on me to accept baptism ceased. I turned twelve, fifteen, then eighteen without being baptized, a fact that scandalized some of the congregation; however, my parents, who openly discussed everything else, never said a word to me. The issue, and the episode that had illuminated it, was surrounded by a clear ring of silence that, for our garrulous family, was something close to supernatural. I continued to go to New African—in fact, continued after Matthew, who dropped out abruptly during his freshman year in college; the ambiguousness in my relations with the old church gave me at times an inflated sense of privilege (I saw myself as a romantically isolated religious heroine, a sort of self-made Baptist martyr) and at other times a feeling of loss that I was too proud ever to acknowledge. I never went up to take my father's hand, and he never commented upon that fact to me. It was an odd pact, one that I could never consider in the light of day; I stored it in the subchambers of my heart and mind. It was only much later, after he died, and I left New African forever, that I began to examine the peculiar gift of freedom my father—whose entire soul was in the church, and in his exuberant, bewitching tongue—had granted me through his silence.

# Mother

In the summer my mother got up just after sunrise, so that when she called Matthew and me for breakfast, the house was filled with sounds and smells of her industrious mornings. Odors of frying scrapple or codfish cakes drifted up the back stairs, mingling sometimes with the sharp scent of mustard greens she was cooking for dinner that night. Up the laundry chute from the cellar floated whiffs of steamy air and the churning sound of the washing machine. From the dining room, where she liked to sit ironing and chatting on the telephone, came the fragrance of hot clean clothes and the sound of her voice: cheerful, resonant, reverberating a little weirdly through the high-ceilinged rooms, as if she were sitting happily at the bottom of a well.

My father left early in the morning to visit parishioners or to attend church board meetings. Once the door had closed behind him, the house entered what I thought of as its natural state —that of the place on earth that most purely reflected my mother. It was a big suburban house, handsomer than most, built of fieldstone in a common, vaguely Georgian design; it was set among really magnificent azaleas in a garden whose too-small size gave the house a faintly incongruous look, like a dowager in a short skirt. The house seemed little different from any other in my neighborhood, but to me, in my early-acquired role as a detective, a spy, a snooper into dark corners, there were about it undeniable hints of mystery. The many closets had crooked shapes that suggested secret passages; in the basement, the walls of the wine cellar—its racks filled by our teetotaling family with old galoshes and rusty roller skates—gave a suspicious hollow sound when rapped; and on the front doorbell, almost obliterated by the pressure of many fingers, was printed a small crescent moon.

The house stayed cool on breathless summer days when tar oozed in the streets outside, the heat excluded by thick walls and drawn shades, and the dim rooms animated by a spirit of order and abundance. When I came dawdling down to breakfast, long after Matthew had eaten and gone plunging off on his balloon-tired Schwinn, I usually found my mother busy in the kitchen, perhaps shelling peas, or stringing beans, or peeling a basket of peaches for preserves. She would fix me with her lively, sarcastic dark eyes and say, "Here comes Miss Sarah, the cow's tail. What, pray tell, were you doing all that time upstairs?"

"Getting dressed."

What I'd been doing, in fact—what I did every summer morning—was reading. Lounging voluptuously in my underpants on the cool bare expanse of my bed, while flies banged against the screen and greenish sunlight glowed through the shades, I would read with the kind of ferocious appetite that belongs only to garden shrews, bookish children, and other small creatures who need double their weight in nourishment daily. With impartial gluttony I plunged into fairy tales, adult novels, murder mysteries, poetry, and magazines while my mother moved about downstairs. The sense of her presence, of, even, a sort of tacit complicity, was always a background at these chaotic feasts of the imagination.

"You were reading," Mama would say calmly when I stood before her in the kitchen. "You must learn not to tell obvious lies. Did you make up your bed?"

"I forgot."

"Well, you're not going outside until you've done something to that room of yours. It looks like a hooraw's nest. Your place is set at the table, and the cantaloupe is over there—we've had such delicious cantaloupe this week! Scrape out the seeds and cut yourself a slice. No—wait a minute, come here. I want to show you how to cut up a chicken."

Each time she did this I would wail with disgust, but I had to watch. The chicken was a pimply yellow-white, with purplish shadows and a cavernous front opening; my mother would set

her big knife to it, baring her teeth in an ogress's grin that made
fun of my squeamishness. "You saw along the backbone like this
—watch carefully; it takes a strong arm—and then you *crack* the
whole thing open!"

In her hands the cave would burst apart, exposing its secrets
to the light of day, and with another few strokes of the knife
would be transformed into ordinary meat, our uncooked dinner.

It was easy for me to think of my mother in connection with
caves, with anything in the world, in fact, that was dimly lit and
fantastic. Sometimes she would rivet Matthew and me with a tale
from her childhood: how, at nine years old, walking home
through the cobblestone streets of Philadelphia with a package
of ice cream from the drugstore, she had slipped and fallen
down a storm drain accidentally left uncovered by workmen. No
one was around to help her; she dropped the ice cream she was
carrying (something that made a deep impression on my brother
and me) and managed to cling to the edge and hoist herself out
of the hole. The image of the little girl—who was to become my
mother—hanging in perilous darkness was one that haunted
me; sometimes it showed up in my dreams.

Perhaps her near-fatal tumble underground was responsible
for my mother's lasting attraction to the bizarre side of life.
Beneath a sometimes prudish exterior, she quivered with excitement in the same way her children did over newspaper accounts
of trunk murders, foreign earthquakes, Siamese twins, Mafia
graves in the New Jersey pine barrens. When she commented on
these subjects, she attempted a firm neutrality of tone but gave
herself away in the heightened pitch of her voice and in a little
breathy catch that broke the rhythm of each sentence she spoke.
This was the voice she used to whisper shattering bits of gossip
over the phone. "When Mr. Tillet died," I heard her say once,
with that telltale intake of breath, "the funeral parlor did such
a poor job that his daughter had to *wire her own father together*!"

My mother, Grace Renfrew Phillips, had been brought up with
all the fussy little airs and graces of middle-class colored girls
born around the time of World War I. There was about her an
endearing air of a provincial maiden striving for sophistication,
a sweet affectation of culture that reminded me, when I was
older, of Emma Bovary. She and her cluster of pretty, light-
skinned sisters grew up in a red-brick house with marble steps
in South Philadelphia. They all played the piano, knew a bit of
French and yards of Wordsworth, and expected to become so-

cial workers, elementary-school teachers, or simply good wives to suitable young men from their own background—sober young doctors, clergymen, and postal administrators, not too dark of complexion. Gracie Renfrew fit the pattern, but at the same time dismayed her family by attending Communist Party meetings, joining a theater group, and going off to a Quaker work camp.

When she married my father, the prescribed young minister, my mother had become, inevitably, a schoolteacher—a beautiful one. She was full-faced, full-bodied, with an indestructible olive skin and an extraordinary forehead—high, with two handsome hollows over the temples. She had a bright, perverse gaze, accentuated by a slight squint in her left eye, and a quite unusual physical strength. She swam miles every summer at the swim club, and at the small Quaker school, where I was a student and she taught sixth grade, it was common to see her jumping rope with the girls, her large bosom bobbing and a triumphant, rather disdainful smile on her face. Her pupils adored her, probably because her nature held a touch of the barbarism that all children admire: she would quell misbehavior, for instance, by threatening in a soft, convincing voice to pull off the erring student's ears and fry them for supper.

At home Mama was a housekeeper in the grand old style that disdains convenience, worships thrift, and condones extravagance only in the form of massive Sunday dinners, which, like acts of God, leave family members stunned and reeling. Her kitchen, a long, dark, inconvenient room joined to a crooked pantry, was entirely unlike the cheerful kitchens I saw on television, where mothers who looked like June Cleaver unwrapped food done up in cellophane. This kitchen had more the feeling of a workshop, a laboratory in which the imperfect riches of nature were investigated and finally transformed into something near sublimity. The sink and stove were cluttered with works in progress: hot plum jelly dripping into a bowl through cheesecloth; chocolate syrup bubbling in a saucepan; string beans and ham bones hissing in the pressure cooker; cooling rice puddings flavored with almond and vanilla; cooked apples waiting to be forced through a sieve to make applesauce; in a vat, a brownish, aromatic mix for root beer.

The instruments my mother used were a motley assemblage of blackened cast-iron pots, rusty-handled beaters, graters, strainers, and an array of mixing bowls that included the cheapest plastic variety as well as tall, archaic-looking stoneware tubs inherited from my grandmother, who had herself been a legendary cook. Mama guarded these ugly tools with jealous solicitude, suspicious of any new introductions, and she moved in her kitchen with the modest agility of a master craftsman.

Like any genuine passion, her love of food embraced every aspect of the subject. She read cookbooks like novels, and made a businesslike note in her appointment book of the date that Wanamaker's received its yearly shipment of chocolate-covered strawberries. Matthew and I learned from her a sort of culinary history of her side of the family: our grandfather, for instance, always asked for calf brains scrambled with his eggs on weekend mornings before he went out hunting. Grandma Renfrew, a sharp-tongued beauty from North Carolina, loved to drink clabbered milk, and was so insistent about the purity of food that once when Aunt Lily had served her margarine instead of butter, she had refused to eat at Lily's table again for a year. My mother's sole memory of her mother's mother, a Meherrin Indian called Molly, was of the withered dark-faced woman scraping an apple in the corner of the kitchen, and sucking the pulp between her toothless jaws.

Mama took most pleasure in the raw materials that became meals. She enjoyed the symmetry, the unalterable rules, and also the freaks and vagaries that nature brought to her kitchen. She showed me with equal pleasure the handsome shape of a fish backbone; the little green gallbladder in the middle of a chicken liver; and the double-yolked eggs, the triple cherries, the peculiar worm in a cob of corn. As she enjoyed most the follies, the bizarre twists of human nature and experience, so also she had a particular fondness for the odd organs and connective tissues that others disdained. "Gristle is delectable," she would exclaim as Matthew and I groaned. "The best part of the cow!"

I was a rather lazy and dunderheaded apprentice to my mother. She could be snappish and tyrannical, but I hung around the kitchen anyway, in quest of scrapings of batter, and because I liked to listen to her. She loved words, not as my father the minister did, for their ceremonial qualities, but with an offhanded playfulness that resulted in a combination of wit and nonsense. In her mischievous brain, the broad country imagery of her Virginia-bred mother mingled with the remains of a ladylike education that had classical pretensions. When she was annoyed at Matthew and me, we were "pestilential Pestalozzis"; we were also, from time to time, as deaf as adders, as dumb as oysters, as woolly as sheep's backs; we occasionally thrashed around like horses with the colic. At odd moments she addressed recitations to the family cat, whom she disliked; her favorite selections were versions of "O Captain! My Captain!" ("O Cat! my Cat! our fearful trip is done . . .") and Cicero's address to Catiline ("How long, Cat, will you abuse our patience? . . .").

On summer evenings, after the dinner dishes had been washed and as the remains of the iced tea stood growing tepid in the pitcher, my mother, dreamy and disheveled, finally would emerge from the kitchen. "Look at me," she'd murmur, wandering into the living room and patting her hair in the mirror over the piano. "I look like a Wild Man of Borneo."

She would change into a pair of oxfords and take a walk with me, or with a neighbor. At that time of day June bugs hurled themselves against the screens of the house, and my father, covered with mosquito repellent and smoking cigarette after cigarette, sat reading under the maple tree. In the diffuse light after sunset, the shadows around the perfectly ordinary houses up and down the street made the unambitious details of their designs—turrets, round Victorian towers, vague half-timbering —seem for once dramatic. All the backyards of the town seemed to have melted into one darkening common where packs of kids yelled faintly and fought their last battles before bedtime. Cars pulled out of driveways and headed for movie theaters or the shopping centers along the Pike, and the air smelled like honeysuckle and onion grass. When Mama and I walked together, we would wander up and down the long blocks until the streetlights came on.

One evening during the summer that I was six years old, we stopped to visit a neighboring family in which something sad and shocking had happened the previous winter. The father, a district judge named Roland Barber, had driven one gray afternoon to the marshland outside the airport and there had shot himself. Judge Barber, a short, grave, brown-skinned man with a curiously muted voice, had been a member of my father's congregation and had served with him on the board of the NAACP. His suicide, with hints of further-reaching scandal, sent a tremendous shock through the staid circles of my parents' friends, a shock that reached down even into the deep waters that normally insulated Matthew and me from adult life. For a few weeks after the suicide we held long grisly discussions on arcane, even acrobatic ways to do away with oneself.

The house in which Mrs. Barber continued to live with her teenage daughter was little different from our house, or any other in our neighborhood: a brick Colonial with myrtle and ivy planted around it instead of grass, and a long backyard that sloped down to a vegetable garden. I knew the Barbers' yard well, because there was an oak tree near the vegetable garden, with a swing in it that neighborhood kids were allowed to use. On the evening my mother and I came to visit, the daylight was fading, and the windows of the house were dark. It seemed that no one was home, but in the summers in our town, people often waited a long time in the evening before turning on lamps. It occurred to me as we walked up the driveway that the house itself seemed to be in mourning, with its melancholy row of blue spruces by the fence; I gave way, with a feeling that was almost like ecstasy, to a sudden shudder. Mama rubbed my goose-pimply arms. "We'll just stay a minute," she said.

My mother was carrying a recipe for peach cobbler. It was intended for Mrs. Barber, a bony woman who had fascinated me even before her husband's death, because she wore a very thick pair of elasticized stockings. However, after we'd knocked and waited for a while, the front door was finally opened by Phyllis, the Barbers' sixteen-year-old daughter. Mama, who had taught Phyllis, sometimes referred to her as "the fair and brainless"; I had seen her plenty of times at the swim club, pretty and some-what fat-faced, drawing the stares of the men to her plump legs in Bermuda shorts. That night, though it was only about eight o'clock, she opened the door in a light summer bathrobe and peered out at us without turning on the porch lights.

"Hello, Mrs. Phillips. Hi, Sarah," she said in a low, hesitant voice. She came out onto the dark steps as she spoke, and let the screen door bang behind her. She explained that her mother wasn't there, and that she had been taking a shower when the bell rang; she radiated a fresh scent of soap and shampoo. When my mother asked her how she was feeling, she answered in the same hesitant tone, "All right."

I looked at her with a kind of awe. It was the first time I had seen her since I had heard the news about Judge Barber, and the first time I had ever stood right in front of anyone associated with an event that had caused such a convulsion in the adult

world. In the light-colored robe, with her wet hair—which normally she wore flipped up at the ends and pulled back with a
band, like other high-school girls in the neighborhood—
combed back from her forehead, she had a mysterious, imposing
look that I never would have suspected of her. I immediately
ascribed it—as I was ascribing the ordinary shadow of the summer twilight around the doorway—to the extraordinary thing
that had happened to her. Her face seemed indefinably swollen,
whether with tears or temper, and she kept her top lip tightly
clenched as she talked to my mother. She looked beautiful to
me, like a dream or an illustration from a book, and as I stared
at her, I felt intensely interested and agitated.

In a few minutes Phyllis went back inside. My mother and I,
as we had done many times before, walked quietly up the Barbers' driveway and through the backyard to the swing in the oak
tree. Mama stopped to pick a few tomatoes from the overloaded
plants in the Barbers' vegetable garden, and I helped her,
though my second tomato was a rotten one that squashed in my
fingers.

It was completely dark by then. Lightning bugs flashed their
cold green semaphores across the backyards of the neighborhood, and a near-tropical din of rasping, creaking, buzzing night
insects had broken out in the trees around us. I walked over and
sat down in the oak-tree swing, and Mama, pausing occasionally
to slap at mosquitoes, gave me a few good pushes, so that I flew
high out of the leaves, toward the night sky.

I couldn't see her, but I felt her hands against my back; that
was enough. There are moments when the sympathy between
mother and child becomes again almost what it was at the very
first. At that instant I could discern in my mother, as clearly as
if she had told me of it, the same almost romantic agitation that
I felt. It was an excitement rooted in her fascination with grotesque anecdotes, but it went beyond that. While my mother
pushed me in the swing, it seemed as if we were conducting,
without words, a troubling yet oddly exhilarating dialogue about
pain and loss.

In a few minutes I dragged my sneakered feet in a patch of
dust to stop the swing. The light of a television had gone on
inside the Barber house, and I imagined fat, pretty Phyllis Barber carefully rolling her hair on curlers, alone in front of the
screen. I grabbed my mother's hand and said, "It's very sad, isn't
it?"

"It certainly is," said Mama.

We took a shortcut home, and by the time we got there, it was time for me to scrub my grimy arms and legs and go to bed. Mama went immediately to the refrigerator and got out an uncooked roast of pork, which she stood contemplating as if it were the clue to something. She smelled of sage and dried mustard when she came upstairs to kiss Matthew and me goodnight.

# Gypsies

Franklin Place, the street that ran like a vein through most of my dreams and nightmares, the stretch of territory I automatically envisioned when someone said "neighborhood," lay in a Philadelphia suburb. The town was green and pretty, but had the constrained, slightly unreal atmosphere of a colony or a foreign enclave; that was because the people who owned the rambling houses behind the shrubbery were black. For them—doctors, ministers, teachers who had grown up in Philadelphia row houses—the lawns and tree-lined streets represented the fulfillment of a fantasy long deferred, and acted as a barrier against the predictable cruelty of the world.

Franklin Place began at the white stucco walls of the swim club, constructed by neighborhood parents for their children, who couldn't swim elsewhere. It ran three tranquil blocks downhill to intersect the traffic of Marymount Lane, a road that traveled through Brandywine country into Delaware. Sometimes in summer, when I listened to the cicadas striking themselves into song from tree to tree, down the street and into the valley, I would imagine following that rasping chorus as it headed south —flying fast over shopping centers, split-level developments, cities, and farms until I reached the perilous region below the Mason-Dixon Line, the region my parents had told me held a sad and violent heritage for little girls like me. Beyond a self-conscious excitement when I heard this, I had little idea of what they meant. For as long as I could remember, the civil rights movement had been unrolling like a dim frieze behind the small pleasures and defeats of my childhood; it seemed dull, a necessary burden on my conscience, like good grades or hungry people in India. My occasional hair-raising reveries of venturing into the netherworld of Mississippi or Alabama only added a voluptuous edge to the pleasure of eating an ice-cream cone while seated on a shady curb of Franklin Place.

One July morning my best friend, Lyn Yancy, and I were playing a great new game in the middle of our street. The game involved standing about twenty feet apart and whacking a large, bouncy red rubber ball back and forth with a pair of old putters that belonged to Doctor Yancy. Most of our time was spent chasing the red ball, which had an eccentric will of its own. Each retrieval was an adventure—from the stand of bamboo in the corner of Reverend Reynolds's yard (counting my father, three ministers lived on the block); from the hazardous green slope in front of the Pinkstons' house, patrolled by a nasty little Scottie named Pattycake; from the pyracantha hedge in front of the house where the Tate twins lived, tough sixth-grade boys who sometimes extorted Sugar Babies from Lyn and me up at the swim club.

It was high midsummer, the season that is unimaginable when you are twining your ankles around the legs of a straight-backed chair in school. All that week the sky had been a fine clear blue, like a direct gaze, and the heat could stop you flat, like a wall, if you were coming out of a cool house. Backyards were full of the raw, troubling odor of tomato vines, and the colony of black ants among the dusty petunias on the slope near the train station had grown into an overcrowded pueblo. If you wore cotton socks with your sneakers and went around riding bikes and hanging from tree branches all day, and you didn't go swimming, when you took off your clothes at night, your legs would be coated with a layer of the outdoors that ended abruptly where your socks had been, and your mother would say, "Run a tepid bath and scrub those legs and show them to me before you even get near the sheets."

Lyn and I whacked the red ball and screeched at each other, and danced up and down the street with the spidery gait of little girls who are rapidly growing taller. We were both seven years old and looked enough like sisters to pretend it almost constantly—two light-bodied, light-skinned little colored girls with our frizzy hair in braids that our mothers had bound into coro-

nets because of the heat. It was fun to run on the broad, newly
paved street that looked like a leafy tunnel crisscrossed with
shafts of greenish sunlight. We were playing mainly in front of
Lyn's house, which was big and made out of stone with mica in
it and had a grape arbor and a fascinating garage that the previous owner had left filled with stacks of Scandinavian nudist
magazines. Occasionally we paused in our game as neighbors
pulled in and out of their driveways. There was Judge Ramsgan-
nett, plump, brown, and silver-haired in his big black car; Lyn's
mother, the dreamy-eyed Mrs. Yancy, on her way to the A&P in
a creaky yellow station wagon; Freddie Monroe, a college junior,
in a little green sports car that seemed to Lyn and me to be the
final word in sophistication.

After a while, wiping our sweaty faces, we sat down on the
curb. We started talking about ponies, and about a scheme I had
to package the mulberries that grew on a tree in my backyard
and sell them to the patients at a nearby hospital. Lyn thought
it was a great idea. "Charge ten cents a bag, and we'll get rich!"
she said, and hitched up her shorts to scratch a mosquito bite
on her thigh.

Down the street came Walter, Lyn's little brother, sucking on
a blue Popsicle.

"Hey, Walter, where'd you get the Popsicle?" I called.

"Good Humor," murmured Walter, slurping. He was a
sturdy-legged boy of five, who, with his bulging brow and pro-
tuberant light-brown eyes, looked a little like a baby dolphin.
The Popsicle, dissolving in the heat, had left a trail of purple
splotches down the front of his Woody Woodpecker t-shirt. He
stopped and regarded us warily.

"Give us a bite," said Lyn.

"No!" exclaimed Walter, jumping as if he'd received an electric shock. He stuck out his bluish tongue at us and ran toward
the house, hopping over our two bicycles, which we'd left in the
driveway.

"I'm gonna tell Mom you were eating before lunch!" Lyn
shouted after him. "And don't you dare drink from the hose
again!"

"He drinks from the hose and gets his clothes disgustingly
wet," she explained to me.

"Disgusting" was one of Lyn's favorite words: just saying it
filled her with such glee that she lay back on the grass beside the
curb and waved her thin legs in the air. I flopped back beside

her, and lay staring up into the branches of the big sugar maple that stood in the Yancys' front yard. It was almost noon, and the sun overhead struck straight down through the green maple leaves, making discs of light that a hot breeze shifted over our faces. In the treetops the cicadas were going wild, stretching their harsh note up into the arid spaces unprotected by shade; around us, near and far, was the drone of a dozen lawnmowers.

I was thinking, with a savoring sort of delight, that soon it would be lunchtime—cream-cheese-and-jelly sandwiches, I hoped—and that in a few weeks my brother, mother, father, and I would leave for the cottage we rented every summer at the beach in New Jersey; and that sometime—not too soon—after that, the leaves on the big maple would turn yellow, and Lyn and I could make a leaf fort the way we had last fall. That was the best fun of all: the ring of leaves heaped up so high it seemed like a castle keep, the cold, brilliant sun of autumn overhead, the smell of smoke from leaf piles burning up and down Franklin Place, and the two of us giggling snug and protected in the center, our hair and clothes full of leaves.

Just at that moment a truck turned onto Franklin Place, and Lyn and I jumped up to get a look at it. Trucks were unusual on our street, and this was the strangest one we'd ever seen: a large battered red pickup, its dusty hood and fenders scarred with patches of rust. It carried in back a high, tangled mass of odd-looking furniture that turned out to be tables and chairs knocked roughly together out of pine branches, the way Lyn and I sometimes made benches for our dolls.

The man behind the wheel had dark skin but was not a Negro; he looked a bit like one of the Indians we saw constantly defeated in TV westerns. He wore a green plaid flannel shirt; his face was a weathered mass of cords and seams, and his oily black hair was slicked back from his forehead. Beside him was a woman with the same kind of ropy brown face, and in the back of the truck, perched in a kind of niche in the furniture, rode a black-haired boy of about fifteen. The truck slowed and stopped beside us.

"Little girls, do you live around here?" the man called out to us.

"Right down the street," I said, and Lyn pointed silently up her driveway.

The woman in the truck opened the door, climbed out, and came around to us. Up close, we could see that her black hair, pulled back in a rough ponytail, was dyed a dry red at the front. She wore a long, faded yellow skirt, rubber sandals, and a gray t-shirt with one of the joke insignias you could get printed at the Atlantic City boardwalk. Hers read "Siberian Salt Mines," and under the loose gray fabric, her long breasts swayed back and forth in a way in which our mothers' well-contained bosoms never did. There was something frightening and wild about the outfit, and about the woman herself; she grinned at us, and we saw that one of her front teeth was broken in half.

"Is this neighborhood all colored?" she asked, in a voice that had an accent to it, and also a tinge of complaint or lament.

"I guess so," said Lyn, almost whispering.

The woman gave a harsh chuckle. "It's a real crime for colored to live like this," she said, putting a hand on her hip and looking up and down the street with small dark eyes that had the same glistening brightness, the jumpy intensity, of the eyes of a crow that had once alighted for an instant on my bedroom windowsill. She said a rapid phrase in a strange language to the man in the truck, and he scowled and spat heavily into the street. The boy in the back of the truck lifted his chin and stared at Lyn and me.

"You are very lucky little girls," continued the woman. "Very lucky, do you understand?"

"We understand," I said. At some point during this exchange Lyn and I had arranged ourselves side by side, and were holding hands tightly.

"When my son was your age, he never got to play like you girls do," said the woman. "He had to work hard; so do I. We get these trees from down in Jersey, and then we make the furniture. Two times, three times, I almost lost a finger from the saw."

The man inside the truck said something sharp to her in the language they shared, and she quickly gave us a broad smile, though her eyes remained the same avid black points. "Do you girls think that your parents would like to buy some furniture?" she asked, changing her voice and waving her hand at the tangle of pine in the back of the truck. "It's for the lawn."

"You'll have to ask my mother," I said, staring past the woman to the place where the man had spat. On the smooth gray paving of the street, it made a wet circle that was vanishing fast in the noonday heat.

Many families in the neighborhood, including mine, bought furniture from the people with the red truck. Gypsies was what they were, my father told us that night at dinner, shaking the ice thoughtfully in his glass of tea. We were eating roast chicken and corn on the cob and garden tomatoes, a magical summer menu, and the air from the kitchen fan was making my mother's hair dance above her face. "They used to come through Philadelphia all the time when I was young," said Daddy. "Crowds of them, first in wagons and then in big old cars. They were tinkers—used to fix pots. It's strange to see them doing this kind of work."

"Do they steal children?" I asked abruptly.

Beside me, Matthew snickered. "They wouldn't want you!" he whispered, poking my foot with his. I ignored him.

"Gypsies stealing children is just an old tale," said my mother. "Sarah, you have to eat all the kernels on the cob, or else you won't get another ear of corn."

"Those Gypsies just seem dangerous to have around the neighborhood," I persisted. "And that lady said that it was a crime for colored to live like this, and after that the man spit in the street."

"Spat," corrected my mother automatically, and she looked over at my father with a wry smile.

"Well, everybody's got . . . to . . . feel . . . better . . . than . . . somebody," said Daddy, drawling his words out progressively slower until they were as slow and exaggerated as the Uncle Remus record we had. He had the compressed look about his cheeks that he got whenever he was about to tell a joke, one of the complicated civil rights jokes he swapped with my light-hearted Uncle Freddy. "Most of the world despises Gypsies, but a Gypsy can always look down on a Negro. Heck, that fellow was right to spit! You can dress it up with trees and big houses and people who don't stink too bad, but a nigger neighborhood is still a nigger neighborhood."

"James! Stop!" said my mother sharply, and Daddy stopped, though he kept the tight look on his face for the rest of the meal. Matthew and I kept glancing at him from the corners of our eyes; we'd never heard him talk that way before.

After dinner I met Lyn down at the swim club. It was the nicest time of day to swim, when the parking lot was almost empty and the shadows from a line of poplars stretched over the cooling grass. While adults chatted quietly in lawn chairs and teenagers began to dance to sentimental records on the jukebox, we played complex underwater games. Around sunset the pool always began to seem a mysterious body of water of undefined dimensions, full of shadows and dim corners; when we lay on our backs and floated, looking up, the evening sky was a tender blue, and the odor of chlorine over everything was a strong, beneficent, healing scent. We were always wonderfully exhausted after these swims, lugging our damp towels home in deep silence through the darkening cricket-lined streets as if the power of speech had been washed out through our pores.

That evening as we were walking home down Franklin Place, we heard the noise of a motor behind us and looked around, surprised to see the red truck. The stack of furniture was much reduced, and the dark-haired boy was standing up, leaning on the back of the cab. The truck paused, its motor chugging like a train engine in the quiet street, and the woman opened the cab door to call out hello to us in a friendlier voice than she had used before. "You went swimming," she said. "Was it fun?"

"It was OK," I said, thinking that if she got out and tried to grab us, I would run up the nearest driveway and pound on the door of Mr. Nansemond, an elderly bachelor from St. Kitts who grew blue hydrangeas.

"You girls want a ride down the street?" asked the woman, and when we said "No," she gave the same kind of harsh chuckle she had given that afternoon. "We're going to drive back to Jersey now, so goodbye to you. Just remember you are lucky little girls to live here."

She slammed the cab door, and the truck roared off into the darkness. I hugged my wet towel and said to Lyn, "They wanted to kidnap us."

"Oh, no they didn't!" said Lyn stoutly. "Don't be such a chicken." But she looked at me with eyes that were very round and bright. For a minute we stood feeling small in the warm summer evening with the big shadowy trees rustling over our heads, and then we took off down the street as if hobgoblins were pursuing us. We gave long, shrill, panicky whoops as we ran, and we didn't stop until we stood safely at our front doors.

The next morning I took a look at the lawn furniture my family had bought from the truck: it was knocked together out of rough, hairy pine logs with a lopsided look and an immediate appeal to spiders and crawling insects. No one in the family ever sat on the furniture, and my mother made a few quips about the "Romany spell" that must have been cast to get her to buy something so worthless; in the winter my father chopped it up for firewood. It was the same for the rest of the neighborhood;

stories of the ephemeral tables and chairs that fell apart during thunderstorms or barbecues became standard jokes up and down Franklin Place. As for me, for several nights in a row I woke up with a jolt, thinking, "Gypsies!"

It was not that I had really feared being stolen: it was more, in fact, that they seemed to have stolen something from me. Nothing looked different, yet everything was, and for the first time Franklin Place seemed genuinely connected to a world that was neither insulated nor serene. Throughout the rest of the summer, on the rare occasions when a truck appeared in our neighborhood, Lyn and I would dash to see it, our hearts pounding with perverse excitement and a fresh desire for alarming knowledge. But the Gypsies never came back.

# Marching

---

Sometimes the suspicion crossed my mind that all adults belonged to a species completely different from my own. One was never quite sure what they cared about, just as it was hard to tell why they laughed, and what kind of laughter it was. The eye of a grownup, like that of a cat or a praying mantis, seemed to admit a different spectrum of light. Compared to my world—a place of flat, brilliant colors, where every image was literal, and a succession of passions grabbed my soul with forthright violence—the atmosphere in which my parents existed seemed twilit, full of tricky nuance.

My father, especially, could be quite confusing. Once, when my family was visiting New York, and Uncle Freddy, who was a lawyer for the NAACP, was taking Daddy, Matthew, and me on a tour of Harlem, Daddy began to talk in a high, affected voice.

"Look at the tenements and the trash!" he said. "I'm awfully glad *I'm* not a Negro, aren't you, Frederick?"

"Oh, yes," said Uncle Freddy in the same kind of voice. "I wouldn't like to be a Negro!"

"But they don't mind the mess as we would," said Daddy. "Negroes are jolly people."

"They're the Happy People!" exclaimed Uncle Freddy, and the two brothers chuckled together, on an odd note. They looked alike as they laughed, though Uncle Freddy, younger, slimmer, more urbane, browner-skinned than my father, with a pair of pale eyes that were like a jolt of electricity in his dark face, was the handsomer of the two.

In the back of the car, I sent a look that was a question over to Matthew. The year was 1959, and I was six and Matthew was nine, and the car was a black Packard with seats of a green and yellow strawlike weave that lit up with a rustic sparkle in the late-spring sunlight. "They're joking, silly—pretending to be white," whispered Matthew. I said nothing, but bent my face into the breeze from the open window and peered at the ruinous streets around us, wondering at the complicated twists in grownup funny bones.

Daddy taught Matthew and me to stick out our chins and say "Negro" with near-military briskness when we spoke of ourselves in the classrooms of our Quaker school, and occasionally he brought home for us stacks of books filled with the strenuous exploits of heroic slaves. When he wasn't preaching sermons, or visiting his parishioners from the New African Baptist Church, he seemed to spend his time in rooms full of men with dark suits —rooms in which the words "civil rights," constantly spoken, took on such gigantic significance that they seemed to be about to emerge from the clouds of cigarette smoke like the title of a Cecil B. DeMille movie. Yet sometimes, when Daddy was sitting quietly with my mother in the evenings, he would talk unflatteringly about Negroes, referring to them as *we*, or *us*. "Yes, that neighborhood has gone downhill, now that *we* have moved in," he would say. "There's nobody like *us* for spoiling a community." And once, when Mama was urging him to make some changes in the garden of our house, he looked at her and said in a withering voice, "You seem determined to make the house vulgar. Do you want it to *look* like it belongs to a colored man?"

When Daddy and I visited Washington in July of 1963, everything was white stone and concrete, and the monuments radiated heat like white-hot stars. Mama was in Europe, and Matthew was braiding lanyards and winning swimming prizes at a Baptist camp in the Poconos, and I experienced the unspeakable, nearly monstrous joy of monopolizing my father. We stayed in a tall, cool brick house that belonged to a trio of elderly ladies, cousins of my father's. They all had heads of tiny serpentined gray curls, and crocheted edges around their washcloths; they fixed paralyzing meals of greens and ham and biscuits, and called Daddy by his middle name. The house had shining floors, and many glass doors that opened in on airless rooms; over the

mantelpiece of an unused fireplace filled with copies of *Ebony*
hung a portrait of my great-great-grandfather, a bony, austere-
looking free mulatto named Amos Twist. The little girl who
lived in the house next door was named Jody, and was a relative
in some way. She had long buff-colored hair strained back in
such tight braids that her eyes seemed to bulge from their sock-
ets. She called her bicycle Lancelot; we spent the simmering
afternoons riding up and down the pavement screeching at each
other. I was absolutely happy.

Some developing project kept Daddy downtown all day, and
when he came back for dinner and hugged my head against his
chest and said, "Hi, Baby," his shirt under his suit jacket was as
wet as if he'd jumped into a swimming pool. Daddy and the
youngest of his cousins sat around the dinner table late into the
night, talking about integration and Dr. Martin Luther King, and
once Cousin Rachel gave me a naughty thrill when she exclaimed, in a piercing voice that I could hear from my bedroom,
"But Forrest"—his middle name was Forrest, and in her
Tidewater accent it became "Farst"—"for Negro ladies, *there's
not a decent public toilet in the District of Columbia!*"

On our way back to Philadelphia at the end of the month,
Daddy and I rode in a cab to Union Station. The driver wore a
small gray cap tilted onto the back of his head; the arm he
draped along the top of the front seat was a rich brown-black,
the color of peat moss, and his voice, rising slowly from his
throat, had a dark, peaty sound. When he found out Daddy was
a minister, he addressed him as "Reverend Doc," and the stories
he told about the senators who rode in his cab made Daddy
shout with laughter. When we came within sight of the station,
the driver whistled a few notes and then said, "Yessir, the District is a pretty empty town in the summer, but in a month or
so, say on the twenty-eighth of August, gon' be a whole lot of
people here, that right, Rev?" He turned his head slightly toward us, so that the corner of his eye showed like a white thread
between his close black lids.

Daddy said, "Going to be a whole lot of people here. A lot of
people marching."

"Amen," said the driver. He stopped at a light and turned his
broad face around completely, so that he and my father could
smile together like accomplices.

Something began to burn and flutter in my chest: it was as if
I had swallowed a pair of fiery wings. The newspapers had been

writing about the great civil-rights march that was to be; I had
heard adults talking about it, and I knew vaguely that that was
why Daddy was in Washington, but all that had been happening
at a distance. Now, suddenly, a tremendous picture appeared in
my mind, as clear and severe in its lighting as one of those old
battle engravings that swarm with distinctly uniformed soldiers
the size of fleas. I saw a million men, their faces various shades
of black, white, and brown, marching together between the blaz-
ing marble monuments. It was glory, the millennium, an ap-
proaching revelation of wonders that made blood relatives of
people like my father and the cab driver. The force of my emotion made me sit up very straight and clench my back teeth; my
stomach, bound in the tight waistband of a plaid skirt, ached
slightly.

Daddy seemed unmoved by the conversation in the taxi; in
fact, at the newsstand in Union Station he began to complain
about the driver. "That son of a gun took an extra dollar twenty-
five!" he said, clutching a Washington *Post* under his elbow and
going through his wallet.

On the train, Daddy studied a letter from his briefcase, read
the paper, and then opened a detective novel titled *Stiffed in San
Remo*. The train went through a tunnel of trees hung with swags
of Virginia creeper and then passed a cornfield where a tow-
headed boy stood waving, his hair bouncing in the breeze like
the corn tassels. I was holding *The Melendy Family,* but I was
thinking about the Crusades and the French Revolution; in my
mind, still reeling with my new vision, rang vague, sonorous
chords of a grand processional.

"I'll go on the march with you," I said to my father.

Daddy marked his place in the novel with his thumb and
looked up. "What?" he said.

"I said I'll go with you on the march."

"Sweetie, that's a great idea," said Daddy. "But it's so far in
the future. Let's think about it when the time comes."

"But I know I want to go!"

Daddy sighed. "Sarah, you know that if you go, Matthew will
want to go too, and I'm not sure that Cousin Rachel will have
room for our family and for Uncle Freddy and Aunt Iz. But we'll
see—we'll ask your mother when she gets home."

Dusty summer air blew in through the window, and I sat back
in my seat feeling the baffled resentment I experienced whenever I ran up against adult obtuseness. From the Crusades to

Cousin Rachel's bedroom space! In a few minutes Daddy looked up again from his reading and patted me on the knee. "My brave girl," he said, looking at me with a certain amount of understanding in his bright little eyes; but I was already angry.

In August my brother and I watched the Washington march on television, the two of us lounging on the creaky green glider that stood on the sun porch at home. As I had known, there had been no question of my going along with my parents: my mother, ever practical, had immediately squelched the idea for fear of stampedes and what she called "exposure"—by which she meant not sun and wind but germs from possibly unwashed strangers. Matthew and I had been confided into the care of evil-tempered old Aunt Bessie, who distrusted most forms of technology and agreed only grudgingly to allow us to turn on the television to see the march.

As we watched, the quiet gray crowd moved down Constitution Avenue and split in half near the end, spreading out like a pair of vast wings in front of the Lincoln Memorial. I strained my eyes at the specks of faces in the procession and imagined my mother and father there, and the mothers and fathers of my friends. Was it grand for them, I wondered, or were they exercising the curious adult talent for considering trivial things in the midst of great? Were they silent, trembling with fervor, or were they exchanging their bitter, complicated jokes about black and white people?

On the screen, the face of Martin Luther King looked very round, with a somber, slightly Eastern air, like a Central Asian moon; when he spoke, his voice seemed to range freely up into the heavens. Matthew, who had recently professed himself a cynic, made fun of me for staring so raptly at the television.

"This stuff doesn't mean anything," he said. "What does this march do? It's not going to help anybody."

I said, "Matty, it's a great thing! It's a symbol. All those people are there because they believe in something. They want to make the world better—isn't it wonderful?"

"Oh, come on, Sarah!" said Matthew, with an annoying superior grin.

We had a big fight about it as we sat there in front of the television. It was an argument in which I came off badly, because, as I found, I wasn't sure what I really thought.

# Servant Problems

Whenever Gretchen and I took our favorite illegal shortcut from the gym to the Great Lodge—a route that took us across one corner of the orchard, past the pruned roses of the Headmistress's Garden, down a brambly alley strewn with cigarette butts in back of the Junior Residence Cottage, and across the bleak gray courtyard where trucks delivered supplies—one of the cooks would wave to us from the back porch outside the school kitchen. The cook was a small, grave, fat man with yellowish-brown skin; he wore a pair of horn-rimmed glasses that gave him an abstracted, professorial air strange to see at lunchtime over a steaming pan of shepherd's pie. In good weather he liked to pass his afternoon break in the open air, on a battered wicker chair that must have dated from the turn of the century, when the Lodge was the summer house of a Wilmington mill owner. Gretchen always waved back to him, her round face pink with democratic enthusiasm, but I knew that the cook's greeting was chiefly for me. His raised arm seemed to offer a kind of hortatory salute that filled me with a mixture of confusion and embarrassment. During my first fall and spring as a day student at the school, I saw him often on the kitchen porch, and I averted my eyes each time.

For sixty years, until the day I arrived there, the Prescott School for Girls had operated on a simple and logical basis: the teachers and students were white, and the domestic staff—a discreet, usually invisible crew of cooks, chambermaids, janitors, and gardeners—was black. This balance was upset when I entered the Prescott seventh grade, a long-legged, eccentric-haired child of eleven—with a mouthful of braces—chafing in the regulation gray worsted tunic and white cotton blouse. I came from a family with a fixed optimism about the brotherhood of man, and I was fresh from the sheltered atmosphere of a tiny Quaker school where race and class were treated with energetic nonchalance. It astonished me considerably to discover a world in which lines were so clearly drawn, and in which I was the object of a discreet, relentless curiosity—a curiosity mingled with wariness on the part of some teachers, as if I were a very small unexploded bomb.

Early in my first month at Prescott, I sat down on my mother's lap after dinner and she asked me what school was like. "Well, it's a little like being in a play," I said. "Everyone's watching me all the time."

I had hoped to make her laugh, but she startled me by bursting into tears. Later I heard her say to my father, "We have to be careful. That school might ruin Sarah."

The main building, or Great Lodge, of the Prescott School was a rambling structure of russet-colored brick, gabled, towered, and turreted, set among modern annexes, playing fields, and groves of horse chestnuts in the rolling hills near the Pennsylvania-Delaware border. The school grounds lay along a wooded ridge that sloped down to Saddler's Creek, a sluggish brown tributary of the Brandywine, on which Prescott girls took out old-fashioned canoes. Confronted directly, Prescott had the absurd charm of any monstrous Edwardian folly, but if you were walking from the train station early on a fall or spring morning, there was a frail, almost unearthly allure to the brick towers rising above masses of foliage. They were the color of sandstone spires in the Arizona desert, and they suggested something so desirable and far off that a glimpse of them over the trees could tighten your heart and make your fingers ache in the pockets of your uniform blazer.

I came to Prescott in the mid-sixties, in an autumn that turned into a long Indian summer. *Life* had recently published pages of pictures showing flames blossoming from storefronts in Newark and Washington, but in the countryside around Saddler's Creek no one was burning anything but leaves. The school grounds stayed green into November, and the senior girls who had sports cars kept the tops down as they had all summer, roaring up and

down Prescott's drive until Miss Cheyney, matron of the boarding school and in charge of administering discipline to day students, punished the offenders by making them attend a special
Saturday study hall; the scandal of that week was that three of
the immured girls, their hair tucked up under floppy Villager
sun hats, had giggled and mugged so outrageously among the
austere cum-laude lists in the study hall that they were suspended. Because of the good weather, Miss Mackintosh,
doyenne of the tough-kneed, brief-kilted Scotswomen who ran
the athletic department, scheduled extra hockey matches, and
the bright fields echoed with shouts of "Sticks!" and the thunder
of hefty legs; mothers with tanned faces shrieked encourage-
ment through the windows of station wagons.

Classes were easy for me, but friends were hard. A few years
earlier I'd seen a picture of a southern black girl making her way
into a school through a jeering crowd of white students, a policeman at her side. Prescott didn't jeer at me—it had, after all,
invited me—but it shut me off socially with a set of almost
imperceptible closures and polite rejections. If one waves a
hand through a tidal pool, one finds the same kind of minute and
instantaneous retreat. The first time I recognized it was in the
seventh-grade locker room; I came in to change out of my sneakers and heard a cheerful din of questions and answers: "What
are you going to wear?" "My blue!" "My green!" "The pink
satin sash!" "The patent pumps from Altman's!"

"Where is everybody going?" I asked Nan Mason, who had
the locker next to mine.

Nan had pinkish hair, pale freckles, and the white eyelashes of
a rabbit. I had often pitied her for being so ugly, but now she
looked as if she pitied me. "To Friday Evening," she said, and
had the grace to drop her eyes. "The dancing class."

"Friday Evening?" I asked, but Nan was looking for something in her locker. For several weeks after that I was certain that
the mothers who organized the Friday Evening dancing classes
for Prescott girls and Newbold Academy boys had simply forgotten to invite me.

Gretchen Manning, my closest friend at school, didn't attend
Friday Evening, either; it was not because she wasn't invited but
because her father, Oswald Manning—famed ban-the-bomb
curmudgeon of the Penn history department—thought it was
nonsense and refused to pay the fee. Gretchen, whose real name
was Margarita, after Bulgakov's heroine, was tall and plump,

with waist-length flat black hair, which she seldom washed, a luminous pink complexion, and a pair of small, sharp hazel eyes. Her uniform tunic, faded and too tight over her expanding breasts, was generally covered with spots of food and of paint from art class and she was lamentably bad at sports. We became friends when we were both assigned to Squad Six, the hockey team for athletic pariahs. In the free-and-easy atmosphere of my former school, I had been considered somewhat of a star of girls' gym, but at Prescott, on the verge of what was to be a quirky and secretive adolescence, I turned into a willful misfit on the playing field, hungry for glory but unwilling to exert myself. I looked with interest at Gretchen, who made her way down the field with a certain monumental grace but a dead slowness.

"I'm an endomorph," she announced the first time she sat down next to me on the leaf-strewn grass (we were awaiting our turns at an exercise—dribble, dribble, dribble, pass). "And you're an ectomorph. That means that no matter what we do we'll never have muscles like those cows out there. What I'd like to do is to join a harem and do nothing but eat Reese's Cups and make love with the caliph once in a while."

"I'd rather join the Navy," I said.

Gretchen stretched out on the grass, propping herself on one round elbow, and peered at me through an oily fall of hair. "My father knows yours," she said. "Your father is James Forrest Phillips, the civil-rights minister. My father is very interested in civil rights, and so am I."

"Don't do me any favors," I said in a tough, snappish voice I had learned from *Dragnet.*

Gretchen looked at me admiringly. "Don't you think it's rather romantic to be a Negro?" she asked. "I do. A few years ago, when Mama and Daddy used to talk to us about the Freedom Riders in the South, my sister Sarabeth and I spent a whole night up crying because we weren't Negroes. If I were a Negro, I'd be like a knight and skewer the Ku Klux Klan. My father says Negroes are the tragic figures of America. Isn't it exciting to be a tragic figure? It's a kind of destiny!"

For the rest of seventh grade, Gretchen and I made a comic duo: the fat and the lean. We were close with the cranky, stifling closeness possible only to a pair of hyper-educated pre-adolescent misfits. We jockeyed for supremacy in the English class taught by the red-haired Miss Whitaker, fresh from Bryn Mawr, and we determined that Gretchen was the philosopher, I the poet. We wept together over Katherine Mansfield stories and, having studied my mother's copy of *Summerhill,* introduced profanity into our conversation so that we could be free children. ("I'm afraid it's too late," said Gretchen. "We're both doomed to frigidity.") We formed a two-member society of revolutionaries, who sang a backward version of the school song and with private signals indicated which members of the Prescott Athletic Association and Charity League would be executed in the first round of purges. Gretchen despised the school and often condemned it, using what she knew of her father's Marxist rhetoric. I aped her, but I had a secret: I wanted to fit in, really fit in, and if Lissa Randolph or Kemp Massie, rulers of the Olympian band of suntanned, gold-bangled popular girls, shimmering in their Fair Isle sweaters, had so much as crooked a finger at me, I would have left Gretchen and followed the way the apostles followed Christ. No one knew my secret—not my parents, who bragged with relief about my levelheaded adjustment; not my brother, Matthew, who might have understood. At night I gloated over a vision of myself transformed by some magical agency into a Shetland-clad blonde with a cute blip of a nickname; reading the Sunday paper, I searched out references to Prescott in the society wedding announcements.

It was Gretchen who introduced me to the secret places at the school: the dusty caverns behind the Flemish tapestries in the Assembly Hall; the muddy bank, downstream from the boathouse, where you could find arrowheads; the heap of fieldstone near the crafts barn that was supposed to cover an Underground Railroad tunnel; the basement under Carroll Theater that held the remains of Prescott stage sets from the twenties and thirties.

After lunch one afternoon, we dared each other to climb up to the top floor of the main tower of the Great Lodge—above the dining hall, the two floors of the Middle School classrooms, and the floor where a few lucky senior boarders had suites. There was no reason for us to do this except that the highest floor was off limits to students: Gretchen and I, good revolutionaries, had the ambition to break every rule in the school at least once. Moving fast to avoid Miss Netherlander, the Argus-eyed old woman who patrolled the halls, we climbed the stairs through the floors of classrooms and the pleasant level full of stuffed animals, ruffled curtains, and Beatles posters that the boarders referred to as Cellblock Ten. One flight above this, we found ourselves in a bare-board corridor where air and light seemed to have been excluded as needless luxuries; there was something mean and meager in the look of the unlit electric bulbs over our heads. We moved cautiously along, peering at narrow doors with numbers on them, until we came to a door that opened onto a room the size of a closet. The room had stained green walls, a small, barred window that seemed grudgingly to allow a view of the back courtyard, a tiny radio on the windowsill, and a black woman seated on the bed.

I was stung by three separate shocks: the deadly bleakness of the room; the fact that people lived on this floor; the fact that contiguous to the bright, prosperous outer life of the school was another existence, a dark mirror image, which, like the other world in a Grimm's tale, was only a few steps off the path of daily routine. I recognized the woman as one of the maids who cleaned the rooms of the boarding students; in a second, she looked up and saw us, the strands of her straightened hair standing out a little wildly around her head, an indecipherable expression in her eyes. Another door opened and another black face looked out. Gretchen and I took to our heels, plunging down the stairs as if we'd just seen a crime.

Gretchen was indignant about the conditions on the top floor of the Lodge, but I tried to forget what we'd seen. Thinking about the black people who worked at the school made me uncomfortable; I didn't know what to feel about them. I put the incident out of my mind, but after that the school reminded me of a print my brother had hanging in his room: it showed a flock of white geese flying on a strong diagonal against a dark sky— except if you looked at it another way it was a flock of dark geese heading in the opposite direction. You couldn't look at the poster and see both without a spinning feeling in your head.

The following September, in eighth-grade English, we dissected *Macbeth,* and Gretchen and I were stagestruck. We bombarded each other with soliloquies each morning when we met on the train to school, and studied from afar the gestures of Miss Wold, the drama teacher, who, with her fluttering Pre-Raphaelite hair and clothes made of murky, nubby fabrics, was the closest thing to a bohemian Prescott could boast. Gretchen and I determined to try out for the Middle School play, which that fall was the Kaufman-Hart comedy *You Can't Take It with You.* Gretchen, who had lost weight over the summer, had set her heart on being Grandpa Vanderhof, and she convinced me that I, with my spidery legs, ballet training, and hysterical laugh, would be perfect for the pixieish dancing daughter, Essie. It is curious that I never questioned the idea. I read for the part on the dusty stage of Carroll Theater and felt something like electricity racing through my body and voice; I drew huge, controlled breaths of excitement, and afterward there was quite a lot of applause from the other girls waiting to audition. Mimsy Davis, a tall, drawling girl whom I admired desperately because she was head of the Middle School Players, came up to me and said, "You know, you were really good!"

I went home that afternoon with a pounding heart and the wild surmise that the gates of paradise were suddenly going to open for me. When the cast list went up the next week, Gretchen, who had auditioned splendidly, did not have a part, but I did: I was to be Rheba. Who was Rheba? Somehow, neither Gretchen nor I could recall her. I leafed through the play and read aloud, "(*From the kitchen comes a colored maid named Rheba—a very black girl somewhere in her thirties. She carries a white tablecloth and presently starts to spread it over the table.*)"

Gretchen snatched the play from me, looked at it, and then threw it on the floor, startling a group of Lower School girls, who stared pertly at us as they trotted by on their way to the playground.

"Pigs!" said Gretchen in a trembling voice as I retrieved the book. She had an operatic way of wringing her plump hands when she was excited or upset. "You're not going to play that part, are you?"

"Of course I'm not," I said. I had to dig my knuckles into my mouth to control a fit of giggling that had seized me; it was laughter that burned my insides like vinegar, and it felt different from any way I had ever laughed before.

That afternoon, throughout Mme. Drouot's eighth-period French class, I was seized by involuntary recurrences of those giggles, so that Madame was cross, and my classmates looked at me strangely—but they had always looked at me strangely.

After that, life at Prescott was easier for me. It was simply, as Matthew remarked when I told him about the play, a matter of knowing where you stood. (I declined the part of Rheba without mentioning the matter to my parents, reasoning, quite rightly, that they would make a fuss.) I had settled into being twelve, and the new way I had learned to laugh seemed to bring me closer to growing up than the small breasts that had appeared with such fascinating suddenness on my chest. In the weeks that followed the casting announcement, when Gretchen and I walked by the cook who waved to us I didn't return his greeting as Gretchen did, but I looked seriously at him, as if he had something to teach me. Over his head, through the yellowing foliage of the chestnut trees, rose the brick towers of the Lodge. As girls' voices floated faintly from the tennis courts and playing fields, I would look up past the top floor and imagine dark geese making a pattern on the sky.

# Matthew
# and Martha

One Sunday there were six of us sitting around the
dining-room table: Daddy, Mama, Matthew, Cousin
Polly, Martha Greenfield, and me. We were eating one
of the extravagant meals my mother could produce in
fits of joy or pique, and because it was a warm spring afternoon
we were drinking ice water from the crystal goblets that had
belonged to Grandma Phillips. When I was very small, I had
liked to tap the thin scrolled edges of those glasses gently and
secretly between my teeth as I drank; the feel of the hard, impossibly delicate crystal seemed to me the feeling of everything
fragile and elegant in the world. Once at Thanksgiving dinner,
however, I had bitten down too hard and ended up with a
mouthful of blood and glass that earned me a trip to the emergency ward and a stitch in the tongue. After that, nothing that
happened at a family dinner could surprise me.

"Will you have another roll?" said Mama to Martha Greenfield. She had a way of looking past Martha when she addressed
her, as if the actual person she was speaking to were standing
six feet farther away.

"No, thank you," said Martha. "They were delicious."

"She eats nothing!" remarked my mother to the table at large,
and Matthew flushed angrily. He opened his mouth to say something, but Martha Greenfield intercepted him, leaning forward
with a smile that won no answer on my mother's face.

"Oh, Mrs. Phillips, you mustn't think that I don't love your food. I've already had two helpings of everything, and I'm afraid a third might be fatal—I might eat four or even five! Matt can tell you that at school I can really make a pig of myself. Isn't that right, Matt?"

"It all goes to your legs, and I hate fat legs," said Matthew, scowling possessively at her across the table. "If you're not careful, young woman, I'll put you on a diet!"

Martha Greenfield made a little moue in Matthew's direction, and I thought, oh, to look like that. She would never need to go on a diet: she was small and slight with a fascinating swiftness to her movements; a fierce vitality gave beauty to her thin face, where the features, taken separately, were a little too strong, too large. Her hair was chestnut-colored and her eyebrows were black, and when she came to visit us, she wore wonderful patterned stockings, bright-colored Italian shoes, and dresses with skirts much shorter than those worn in Philadelphia in the late sixties. She was from New York and, like Matthew, was a freshman at Swarthmore.

At the table she was seated with her back to a buffet that held an elaborate silver tea set. The set had been given to my father by the congregation of the New African Baptist Church to mark his tenth anniversary as minister; above it hung an enormous and hideous painting done in the twenties by an aunt of Daddy's, who had claimed to be one of the lights of the Harlem Renaissance. The painting had a massive, faded gilt frame and depicted two French dolls—a black pickaninny and a white lady of fashion —lolling loose-jointedly against each other on a velvet stool. The effect was Gothic; Matthew had long ago named the picture "The Coon and the Courtesan," and its somber presence had dominated the striped wallpaper of the dining room for as long as I could remember. Sitting in front of it in a short tuniclike spring dress printed with orange flowers, Martha Greenfield looked as if she belonged to a different universe.

"What did you kids do this afternoon?" asked my father, helping himself to more baked squash. Mama had provided a surfeit of vegetables, as if she wanted us all to die of apoplexy: besides the squash there were string beans, collard greens, asparagus, eggplant casserole, pickled cucumbers, and sweet potatoes.

"They didn't go to church, that's certain," mumbled Cousin

Polly, her mouth full of cucumber, which she was chewing cautiously. Cousin Polly was an ancient, opinionated, and nearly blind cousin of my mother's, who came to Sunday dinner every week.

Matthew looked over at me and made the grimace with his mouth that in our private childhood language meant "Adults are idiots" or "Let's get out of here" and usually signified both. I grimaced back at him, trying not to worship him too much. Since going away to college last fall he had changed from a round-cheeked kid who looked about twelve to a tall, bony young man with a mass of frizzy curls tumbling over his high forehead and a handsome thin face that was alternately tense and vibrant.

"Martha and I went with Sarah down to the art museum," said Matthew in a patient voice. "There was a free concert down on the parkway."

"A rock-and-roll concert?" asked Daddy, his little dark eyes gleaming with earnest interest. I had to admit that on these difficult weekends when Matthew brought Martha home, he really did try to make things pleasant. "Did you have a good time, Sair?"

"Yeah, it was great," I said. Actually it had been a sort of misery for me to be there, a skinny overgrown fourteen-year-old among all the hippies and the dashing revolutionary types, and the loving couples kissing and smoking dope to the strains of electric guitars. I had tagged behind Matthew and Martha, who had strolled along talking earnestly about Vietnam, and about their plans to work for a black-voter-registration campaign that summer in Mississippi. They'd constantly been pointing out other interracial couples, laughing smugly, as if they all belonged to a sophisticated club. Later we'd walked down the river, past the faded pink neoclassical buildings that had been the old Philadelphia waterworks and aquarium, under the budding sycamores, to a little pillared pavilion, where Matthew had grabbed Martha and said, "Hello, beautiful!" and my heart had ached with jealousy and with the shame of being fourteen and so ungainly that no one would ever love me.

"I don't like the music they play these days," said Mama.

"I agree with you, Grace," said Cousin Polly. "It's just a hooting and a carrying-on!"

"Did you visit the museum?" Daddy asked Martha.

"Unfortunately not," said Martha. "Matt dragged me away just as I was about to dash in to see the Gauguin murals."

"Well, I brought you to dinner here," said Matthew. "This is a kind of museum."

"That's a nice thing to say about your own home," said Mama.

"It's true," said Matthew.

"Mrs. Burrell," said Martha to Cousin Polly, "Matt tells me that your family comes from Virginia. What part?"

Cousin Polly blinked and laid down her fork. In spite of her age, she was tall and erect and had a lovely length of bone in her wrists, her legs, and her gnarled fingers. The skin of her arms had a corded and wrinkled overlay that reminded me of barnacles, but her face was remarkably unlined—probably because like many colored women of her generation, she was vain of her skin and protected it from the sun. Her eyes were covered with a bluish film, and when she looked at me and spoke in her dry southern voice, I felt that I was talking to a living fossil, one of the Paleozoic creatures that are periodically discovered in deep waters.

"I was raised in Suffolk," she said. "That's by the North Carolina state line. My daddy was a blacksmith, and we had a farm. Papa was born back in slavery times, but he was free and his daddy was free because his granddaddy was a white man. I didn't come to live in Philadelphia until nineteen and twenty-two."

"That's fascinating," said Martha. "Matt, you should do a black history project on your family. It would be incredible!"

"I don't like that word 'black,' " said Cousin Polly. "Colored folks used to think that word was an insult!"

"It's what kids are saying now," said Daddy hastily. "Martha didn't mean any insult. By the way, Cousin Polly, didn't you have a sister named Martha?"

The bluish, rheumed eyes grew thoughtful. "We used to call her Mattie. She married a big, stout fellow named Hubley Turner."

Mama had signaled to me to clear the plates, and now she was cutting into a large peach cobbler. "Martha, your name is unusual for your background, isn't it?" she said to Martha Greenfield.

Martha laughed. "Do you mean that Martha is an unusual name for a Jewish girl?" she said, giving my mother a mischievous, sparkling glance. "I'll tell you the family legend about how I got it. My father's people came here from Odessa in the twenties, and my father, who was a child, was so excited by America that he vowed to name his children after George and Martha Washington. My brother escaped, but here I am!"

"And how does your family like the American boy you've chosen?"

I groaned. Matthew threw down his fork. "Will you lay off, Ma?"

Daddy sent Mama a warning look, but Mama's face was set like stone under her curly dark hair. "I suppose I can ask a simple question if I want to," she said. "I expect that Martha's parents are probably wondering the same thing that we are: why it is that their children can't stick to their own kind."

Matthew put his hands on the edge of the table and pushed his chair back so that the ice rattled in all the glasses. He was sitting directly underneath the faint water stain left on the dining-room ceiling from the time the tub in the Green Bathroom overflowed. The ceiling had been repainted so that only a shadow of the stain remained, but years before, when it was fresh, Matthew and I had lain on our backs on the dining-room rug and pretended that the wavering brownish line outlined an unknown continent, peopled with dinosaurs and comic-book heroes. We were explorers, trekking across lava fields and through swamps filled with pterodactyls.

Matthew was talking to Mama in a fierce voice that threatened, horribly, to become a shout or a tearful howl. "I don't believe you!" he said. "You are just incredible! You and Daddy spend all of your lives sending us to white schools and teaching us to live in a never-never land where people of all colors just get along swell, and then when the inevitable happens you start talking like a goddam Lester Maddox!"

"Shame on you, swearing at your mother like that!" said Cousin Polly.

"I know what I think is right," said Mama in a wobbly voice. In fact it was clear that at that moment she knew nothing at all. The air was filled with a sense of mistakes being made right and left, and with a dreadful muddled array of passions.

Daddy had lit a cigarette, something he usually never did during meals, and now he stubbed it out on the edge of his dessert plate—something else he never did—and leaned forward, the bald spot on his head glistening under the lights. He said, "Matthew, your mother and I are simply concerned about your happiness and Martha's happiness. You two are very young, and the world is not what we all would like it to be."

"And I suppose you'd like me to wait around till it improves! You're a fine advocate for civil rights—like to set up segregated facilities in your own house!" Matthew's voice was cracking hideously, and he suddenly stood up from the table, looking very tall and skinny in his jeans and sweatshirt. "I was a fool to think I could get you guys to behave like human beings," he said in a quieter voice. "You insult me, and you insult Martha, and I'm not going to take it anymore. Don't worry, you'll see me again. But this Sunday dinner is definitely over."

He walked around to where Martha was sitting, her face pale and her lips parted. In a minute they had walked out of the dining room, out the front door, and we heard the sputtering sound of the ancient white Volvo that Matthew had bought from his roommate.

"Young jackass," said Cousin Polly. "Why can't he find a nice colored girl?"

My mother, who had tears on her cheeks, let her forehead drop until it touched the tablecloth. Then she raised her head and suddenly turned to me. "Don't sit there staring—go to your room!"

The order was so violent that it was clearly not meant to be obeyed. I went outside and sat down on the front steps. From inside I could hear the monotonous sound of my parents' voices in argument.

Around me the neighborhood yards were bright green in the late afternoon sunlight, and everything was in bloom: the tough old azalea bushes my father fertilized with oak leaves every fall, the hyacinths my mother, kneeling on a stack of magazines and wearing a ragged jacket of Daddy's, had planted the previous September. Under the azalea bushes to either side of the front steps were the dark passageways that Matthew and I had used in childhood games that never saw the light of day. Whole empires of Martians—represented by pine needles and the minute round seeds of the arborvitae—had risen and been destroyed in that leafy shadow; it was there that we brought the few cigarettes we stole from Daddy's bureau, and there that Matthew, after swearing me to secrecy on pain of instant and horrible death, had built a fire and roasted a dead mouse.

Peering into the darkness under the tall blossoming bushes, I could clearly picture Matthew at nine, knobby-limbed in a baggy pair of shorts and a Davy Crockett t-shirt, his head nearly shaven for summer, his eyes narrowed with diabolical excitement as he impatiently outlined a scheme to me. Sometimes he would bury a tennis ball in the leaves by the front steps and then grab me to explain hastily, "We're saboteurs, and I just planted a deadly explosive that's gonna blow the fort sky-high! That means it's a bomb, dumbbell! It's going to explode, and we have to run for it!" Then he'd be off down the tree-lined street, his face a blurred speeding star, yelling, "Come on, Sarah! Run for your life!" Often in his impatience at playing with a little sister, he would round the corner in the direction of his friend Eddie Ratcliff's house, and I would see him no more that day. But I would keep running after him until my short legs gave out. That was the way it always went: Matthew set the explosions and ran, and I, pulled by some invisible cord, followed after because there seemed to be nothing else to do.

The voices in the dining room had quieted, and through the screen door I heard the slight clatter that meant the table was being cleared. Daddy came outside with the roto-comic section of the Philadelphia *Inquirer* under his arm. "Better go help your mother," he said in a neutral voice, and I dusted off the seat of my blue jeans and went inside. In the dining room I picked up all six of Grandma Phillips's water glasses—the one Martha Greenfield had used, the one at Matthew's place, and the other four—and carried them dangling loosely by the stems, three to a hand, into the kitchen. It was a gesture, I thought; if I'd had the courage, I'd have thrown them all against the wall.

"What in the name of common sense are you doing?" said Mama, who was helping Cousin Polly to wrap up the uneaten peach cobbler. "Put those down, and do it carefully. You kids are going to kill me!"

I looked at her and put the glasses down slowly.

"She's crazy like her brother!" said Cousin Polly.

# The Days of the Thunderbirds

W hen the Thunderbirds arrived at Camp Grayfeather, Ellen, Chen-cheu, and I were waiting for
them, lounging on the splintery steps of the recrea-
tion hall. Behind us a big fly with a weary August
note to its buzz banged against the screen door. In front of us,
under a level evening sun, the straw-colored Delaware countryside—pointedly referred to as "Wyeth Territory" in the camp
catalogue—rolled off from our own wooded hillside toward the
bluish haze that was Maryland. It was a Tuesday and just after
dinner, the tranquil period in a camp day when the woods are
filled with the soft clanging of bells announcing evening activities and the air still holds a whiff of tuna casserole. After dinner
was supposed to be journal-writing time for the three dozen or
so fourteen-year-olds who made up the rank and file at
Grayfeather, but Chen-cheu, Ellen, and I had slipped out of our
tent in order to witness the coming of the Thunderbirds. It was
an event we were awaiting with the same kind of horrified delight as that with which biblical adolescents—as deep in glandu-
lar boredom as we ourselves were—must have greeted a plague
of serpents. The Thunderbirds were a black teenage gang, one
of many that battled in the close brick streets of Wilmington,
and through some obscure adult arrangement they were coming
to spend a week with us at camp.

"Do you think they'll have knives, Sarah?" Chen-cheu asked
me, rubbing an array of chigger bites on her ankle.

Chen-cheu was the camp beauty, a Chinese-American girl from Oberlin, Ohio, whose solid-cheeked, suntanned face had an almost frightening exotic loveliness above her muscular swimmer's shoulders. She had, however, a calm, practical personality that belied her thrilling looks, and she talked with a flat midwestern accent, as if she'd been brought up in a soddy.

"Nah," I said. "Gangs use guns these days."

In fact my only knowledge of the habits of gangs came from seeing the movie *West Side Story,* but like the other black kids at Grayfeather, most of us the overprotected or horribly spoiled products of comfortable suburban childhoods, I had been affecting an intimate knowledge of street life ever since I'd heard about the Thunderbirds.

"Maybe we'll end up massacred," said Ellen in a hopeful voice, unwrapping a stick of gum.

Ellen was always chewing gum, though it was against camp rules; she had come to Grayfeather with about a thousand packages of Wrigley's hidden in her trunk, and even, to the derision of her bunkmates, made little chains of the wrappers. She chewed so much that her father, a Reform rabbi in Baltimore, once made her walk around a shopping mall with a wad of gum stuck to her forehead. She and Chen-cheu and I had been close friends all summer, a brisk female triumvirate who liked to think of ourselves as Maid Marians, both lawless and seductive. (In reality it was only Chen-cheu who provided the physical charms, since Ellen and I were both peaky, bookwormish types.) The three of us made a point of being on the spot whenever anything interesting or scandalous happened at the camp, and the arrival of the Thunderbirds was certainly the most riveting event of the summer.

They were not the first visitors we'd had at Grayfeather: already we'd played host to a morose quartet of Peruvian flute players and a troop of impossibly pink-cheeked Icelandic scouts. The Thunderbirds represented, however, the most ambitious attempt to incarnate the camp motto, which was "Adventures in Understanding." As Ellen once remarked, instead of being a tennis camp or a weight-loss camp, Grayfeather was an integration camp. The campers, most of whose fathers were professors, like Chen-cheu's, or clergymen, like mine, had been carefully selected to form a motley collection of colors and religions, so that our massed assemblies at meals, chapel, and campfires looked like illustrations for UNICEF posters.

It was at chapel the previous Sunday that Ned Woolworth, the camp director, had announced the coming of the Thunderbirds.

"During the next week you'll be more than just kids relating to kids," he said, strolling up and down between the rows of split-log benches, scanning our dubious fourteen-year-old faces with his benign, abstracted gaze, his big gnarled knees (his nickname was Monster Legs) working below his khaki shorts. Woolworth was tall and looked like Teddy Roosevelt, and had an amazing talent for not knowing things. He ignored the generally unenthusiastic silence as his campers coldly pondered the ramifications of doubling up in tents with their comrades-to-be, and passed over the muttered lamentations of the camp misfit, a Nigerian diplomat's son named Femi. He read us a few lines from *The Prophet* and then told us we would be like ambassadors, bridging a gap that society had created. It appeared that the staff had already written and gotten permission from all of our parents.

The arrival of the Thunderbirds at Grayfeather was signaled by a grinding of gears and a confused yelling from far down the dirt road that led through six miles of woods to the camp. As Ellen, Chen-cheu, and I poked one another in excitement, a battered yellow school bus covered with a tangle of long-stemmed graffiti rattled into the clearing and swerved into the dusty parking lot beside the rec hall. The bus ground its gears once more, shuddered, and seemed to expire. The doors flew open, and the Thunderbirds poured down the steps into the evening sunlight.

"They're so *small!*" Ellen whispered to me.

There were ten boys and seven girls—the girls forming, as we later found out, a sort of auxiliary unit to the Thunderbirds— brown-skinned teenagers with mature faces and bodies and stunted, childish legs that gave the boys, with their muscular shoulders and short thighs, the look of bantam cocks.

One of the boys came up to Chen-cheu, Ellen, and me and stood rocking on his heels. "Hello, ladies," he said. "My name is Marvin Jones." He wore tight black pants and a green t-shirt that was printed with the words KING FUNK, and he had an astonishing Afro pompadour that bobbed like a cresting wave over his mobile trickster's face. Above his left eye he had dyed a platinum streak in his hair, and down one brown cheek ran a deep scar.

Looking at him, I had the feeling that something unbelievable was happening in front of me. "Hello," said Chen-cheu, Ellen, and I in a faint chorus.

In a minute Ned Woolworth and the rest of the staff were there organizing things. The sleepy little camp clearing with its square of sun-bleached turf and its cluster of low green-painted buildings seemed suddenly frantic and overcrowded. Radios weren't allowed at Grayfeather, but one of the Thunderbirds had brought a big portable receiver that filled the air with a Motown beat. Martha and the Vandellas were singing, their shrill, sweet voices crackling with static, and the Thunderbirds were bouncing to the beat while they eyed the camp, shoved one another, picked up their abbreviated luggage, and shouted back and forth. Meanwhile, the rest of the Grayfeather campers had slipped unobtrusively, even furtively, out of the woods, like an indigenous tribe showing itself to explorers; they settled on the steps and porches of the rec hall to swing their feet and observe. Little Nick Silver, a math whiz from Toughkenamon, Pennsylvania, who at a precocious twelve years old was the youngest kid at camp, sat down next to me. "You have *got* to be joking," he whispered. "They'll eat us for breakfast!"

With the Thunderbirds had come a counselor from the social agency that had sponsored their visit: a tall, sallow white man with thinning curly hair and a weary, skeptical way of regarding the woods, the camp buildings, the evening sky, and his charges. He talked with Ned Woolworth for a few minutes and then climbed back inside the battered school bus, turning around only once to smile sardonically at the Thunderbirds. "See you later, guys," he called out. "Behave yourselves." The Thunderbirds responded with a kind of roar, and then the school bus started up with another wrench of gears and rattled off through the trees.

Once the newcomers had filed down the path into the woods to put their bags away in the tents, one of the counselors rang the evening activities bell. "We'll have introductions at campfire," she announced. "Be friendly!"

We campers simply looked at one another. With the Thunderbirds gone from the clearing, a powerful current of noise and energy had suddenly been shut off. Bats flitted across the darkening sky, and a breeze from the lake carried a smell of damp leaf mold. While the others were lining up, I went over to inspect a far corner of the dining hall, where I'd seen a group of the Thunderbirds clustering. There, carved deeply into the green paint, was a miniature version of the same long-stemmed, weirdly elegant graffiti that had covered the school bus, and that I had seen spray-painted on decrepit city buildings. It read: T-BIRDZ RULE.

Marvin Jones was the leader of the Thunderbirds. At the get-acquainted campfire, it was his command that galvanized his troops into standing up and stepping forward, one by one, to give their names. ("L.T." "LaWanda." "Doze." "Brother Willy.") He himself stood in the firelight with a crazy tremor running through his body, wearing a rubber-lipped showman's smirk, like a black Mick Jagger. ("Stretch." "Chewy." "Belinda." "Guy.") In the bright circle of hot moving light that baked our faces and knees and left our backs chilled with the damp breath of the big pine grove behind us, we campers studied the Thunderbirds and they studied us. Both groups had the same peculiar expression: not hostility, but a wary reservation of judgment. As bits of ash danced like a swarm of glowing insects in the draft of the fire—a big log-cabin fire, built specially for the occasion by the Wood Crafts class—Ned Woolworth, his cheerful freckled wife, Hannah, and the rest of the staff guided us all through a number of cheers and folk songs.

Most of the counselors looked eager and uneasy. The near-instantaneous grapevine among the campers had already reported that the Thunderbirds had got into trouble immediately after their arrival, as they walked down the path to the boys' tents. Marvin Jones and two others had shinnied up a tall, skinny tree—one of the birches unusual in that area, and beloved by the Nature counselors—swinging on it and pulling it down with their combined weight until it bent over and seemed likely to break. When one of the counselors asked them to stop, Marvin Jones, laughing crazily and hanging on to the birch, responded, "This is the *woods,* man! Ain't *no* law against climbing no tree in the woods!"

That night the Thunderbird girls who had been assigned to share our tent refused to undress until the light was turned out. There were three of them: a pair of tiny, frail-boned sisters named Cookie and June, who had large almond-shaped eyes, hair done identically in an elaborately braided puff over each ear, and small breasts in sharp brassieres that stuck out like pointed Dixie cups through the clinging nylon of their blouses; and Belinda, a stocky girl who looked twenty years old and had a slight squint, straightened hair bleached a bright orange-red in the front, and a loud, unbridled tongue—I had heard Belinda laughing and cursing above the others when they got off the bus. She was subdued now, as were Cookie and June, the three of them sitting bolt upright on the tightly stretched army blankets and sheets of the cots that had been set up for them, muttering replies to the kindly chitchat of our counselor, Molly. Molly was from Jamaica, a student with an anxious plump face and a delightful habit of shaking her head at her campers and exclaiming, "Girls, you are becoming hardened in your ways!"

The three Thunderbird girls responded to Molly with a sudden opacity of gaze, glances among themselves, and abrupt fits of shy giggling. We campers were stricken with shyness ourselves: there was none of our usual roughhousing or bedtime ballets in our underwear, or wisecracking about Patty Haas's ugly boyfriend—a standing joke. Instead we undressed quickly in our bunks, turning away from each other, painfully conscious of the contrast between the elaborately equipped trunks from which we drew our pajamas and the small vinyl bags that our guests had brought. Once Molly had turned off the single yellow bulb that illuminated the tent and had strolled off up the path to a late-night staff meeting at the rec hall, the tent was unnaturally silent.

I arranged myself on my lumpy top bunk as I always did—with the sheet over my head to keep off mosquitoes—and breathed in the scent of slightly mildewed canvas from the rolled sides of the tent. From the bunk beneath me, Chen-cheu, a sound and instant sleeper, gave an adenoidal snore, and I could hear little clicks and rustlings that meant that the Thunderbird girls were undressing. There was a cool breeze blowing with a steady rushing sound in the trees, and I wondered what the girls from the city were thinking as they listened, perhaps for the first time in their lives, to the noises of the wild night. Never had I been so aware of the woods as a living place around me: over the stubborn saw of the crickets, I heard two hoots from a white-faced owl who lived in a tree near our tent, and a gradually intensifying gray light in the direction of the lake meant the moon was rising. In my mind the moon mingled with the yellow school bus that had brought the Thunderbirds, and then I found myself sliding quickly out of the vision, knowing that I'd been asleep. What had awakened me was a soft voice; it was the new girl, June, calling out to her sister in a whisper.

"Cookie—Cookie—are you up? I hear a noise."

There was a soft creak as Cookie got up and crept over to her sister's cot. I leaned my head out slightly from my bunk and in the dim moonlight caught a glimpse of the tiny girl, her hair greased and braided for the night, dressed in her underwear. It hadn't occurred to me until then that perhaps the Thunderbird girls didn't have pajamas. "Hush, girl," hissed Cookie to her sister, sitting lightly down on the cot. "Hush up! You want these bitches to hear you?"

"But there's a noise," whimpered June.

"Hush up, girl. It's just trees, that's all. Just trees."

There was silence, and when after a few minutes I edged my head out of the bunk to have another look, I saw that Cookie had lain down on her sister's cot and that the two girls were sleeping with their heads close together on the pillow.

At breakfast Ned Woolworth announced to a chorus of groans from the campers that instead of swimming or canoeing or tennis, we would divide up into small groups for what he called "rap sessions." My group included Ellen; Jackie Murdock, a camper notorious throughout Grayfeather for his prolonged belches at mealtimes; a plump, round-faced Thunderbird named Ricky; and a skinnier Thunderbird named Les, who wore a peculiar rust-colored bowler hat. There was also Marvin Jones, the Thunderbird leader, wearing an army fatigue jacket open to show his gleaming bronze chest; he sat slumped, wiggling his feet, on his face an expression of exaggerated forbearance.

The six of us, with a counselor, met in a grove of pin oaks near the chapel. It was one of those clear, dry, autumnal days that occasionally leap ahead of their time into the middle of August. The sky was a sharp blue, crisp moving shadows checkered the ground, and in the eyes of all of the kids sitting there was a skittish, inattentive look, as if they might dash off suddenly into the breezy woods.

A green acorn plopped down near Ricky, the plump Thunderbird sitting beside Ellen. "Wha's that?" he asked her, pointing.

"That's an acorn," said Ellen scornfully, tossing back her red hair. "Didn't you ever see an acorn before?"

"No, Sweet Thighs," said Ricky, giving her a lascivious, cherubic smile that showed a broken front tooth. He picked up the acorn and put it carefully into his pocket.

The counselor in charge clapped her hands. She was a diving coach with a pugnacious sunburnt face and a blunt, bossy way of talking. "This morning we're going to discuss friendship,"

she said. "We all have friends, so let's talk about them—who
they are, and what they mean to us—"

"I don't have friends," interrupted Marvin Jones.

"What?" said the counselor.

"I said I don't have friends," said Marvin Jones, looking at her
seriously, the platinum streak in his hair glittering in the sunlight through the treetops. "Yeah, that's right, miss. I mean, shit
—'scuse me, miss—I got my *men*. Spike is my *man*. Ricky is my
*man*, and J.T., that dude with the sunglasses and the 'Free Africa'
t-shirt, he's my *main* man. I mean, them dudes will cut for me.
But they don't be no *friends*. And then we got the Thunderbird
Queens—I mean our ladies."

"*They're* not your friends, of course." said the counselor
acidly.

"No, like I said, we don't have no friends. We got enemies,
though: the Twelfth and Diamond Street gang. You ever hear
of them?"

"No."

"Well, that's good, 'cause the T-birds are on top. Wait a
minute—I'll show you something."

He gave a curt, imperious nod to Ricky and the other Thunderbird beside him, and an odd tension seemed to seize all three
of them. The woods seemed very quiet for a minute. All at once,
synchronized, they stood up, snapping their fingers. In high,
plaintive voices they broke into words and rhythms that were not
quite a song, not quite a chant.

"What the word / Thunderbird . . ."

It was a strange mixture: a bit of Motown, a bit of the inter-
locking verses all kids use to choose sides for games, a bit of the
bouncy silliness of football and basketball cheers, all bound
together quite naturally with swearwords—words that we
Grayfeather campers all knew and used enthusiastically among
ourselves, in spite of what parents and teachers and counselors
had to say. The Thunderbird song could have been ridiculous,
but instead it was thrilling, carrying with it, to those of us who
sat listening, all the resonance of a dangerous young life in the
city. It was clear that the song was not intended as an entertain-
ment for us, but was presented as a kind of credential, like the
letters scratched into the paint of the rec hall.

Ellen and I punched each other excitedly in the ribs and tried
to remember every word. When the song was finished, Marvin

Jones and the other two Thunderbirds flopped down abruptly at the base of a tree, their faces full of restrained pride.

"That was great, fellows," said the counselor. She was trying to seem cordial, but it was clear that she was uncomfortable, almost angry, about what had just happened. "Let's see if you can do a little more talking now, so that we can get to know you."

Marvin Jones picked up a twig from the ground and tapped the toes of his sneakers with it—one, two, three. "Lady, you just got to know us," he said.

Down at the lake that afternoon, Jimmy Terkel, the boating counselor, gave a short briefing on canoeing to an assembled group of campers and Thunderbirds. Terkel was a dark, soft-spoken young man who loved the little irregular lake, with its cedar water and clustering lilies; all summer he had made canoeing into an austere rite, embarking on solitary voyages at dawn or sunset, an angular silhouette at the far corner of the water. The afternoon had grown overcast, and as Terkel talked about water safety and demonstrated the proper way to dip and feather a paddle—the lecture was chiefly for the newcomers, since the campers had been handling canoes all summer—swarms of audacious gnats made forays at our eyes and ears. Suddenly, in the middle of the talk, Marvin Jones strode over to one of the aluminum canoes on the shore and began to push it toward the water. "I want to go for a ride, mister," he said politely to Jimmy Terkel. "I know how to do this. I see it all the time on TV."

Three other Thunderbirds grabbed paddles and rushed over to the canoe, pushing it through the shallows to deeper water and tilting it dangerously when they all climbed in, about fifteen yards from shore. "That's too many in a boat, fellows!" called Jimmy Terkel, coming forward. The gunwales of the overloaded canoe were riding about six inches above the surface of the lake, and the boat shipped water occasionally as the passengers thrashed about trying to position themselves; miraculously, the canoe did not capsize. There was an argument between two of the Thunderbirds ("You on my *arm*, man!") and then the canoe took off with an irregular splayed motion as Marvin Jones and a second Thunderbird paddled with great splashing thrusts.

"Oh, *no*!" Jimmy Terkel muttered, glancing automatically at the heap of orange life preservers on the shore. But no disaster occurred. The canoe made its awkward, lunging way into a cluster of lily pads, and we heard the delighted yells of the novice

canoeists as they yanked up the tough-stemmed blossoms, an act
that the camp staff, ardent conservationists all, had raised in our
minds to the level of a felony. Then the boys in the boat all took
off their shirts, and Marvin Jones stood precariously upright to
paddle like a gondolier, a big lily coiled dripping around his
neck. There was something barbaric and absurd about the sight
of him paddling that overloaded canoe, which, as it wobbled
heavily over the dark water, seemed a parody of a boat, something out of a nursery rhyme. As I watched it, there came to me
out of nowhere a surge of pure happiness. The other campers
seemed to feel it as well; the faces of the kids around me were
contorted with crazy laughter, and some of them were jumping
up and down. Out of the corner of my eye, I saw one of the boys,
from pure *joie de vivre,* as it were, pick up a handful of sand and
rub it into the hair of his bunkmate. Just for a minute, it seemed
that the camp was a place where any mad thing could happen.
While Jimmy Terkel stood on the shore with an angry smile on
his face, campers and Thunderbirds alike were almost dying
with glee. We laughed as if we'd never seen anything so funny.

That was the last, really the only, good time we had with the
Thunderbirds. Later that afternoon a scuffle broke out near the
camp infirmary between two of the gang members and a stable-
boy. A burly counselor from Honolulu broke up the fight, which
was just a matter of shoving and name-calling. The participants
were made to stand face to face and explain themselves, and in
the process they quite spontaneously shook hands and apolo-
gized. In ten minutes the camp grapevine had telegraphed news
of the scuffle to all parts of Grayfeather. It seemed that everyone
involved in the fight had laughed it off except for Ned Woolworth, who rushed to the scene and glared at the three boys as
if he wanted to knock them all down.

The staff had scheduled a hayride for that night. Normally, the
campers looked forward to hayrides: the dusky country roads,
shrill with insects; the creaky wagon and plodding, pungent
horses; the deep, scratchy hay that offered the opportunity for
a little romantic improvisation (though Grayfeather, a camp of
overeducated fourteen-year-olds, was notoriously backward in
that department). That particular evening, a subtle intelligence
flashed through the ranks of the campers, a kind of mass intui-
tion that suggested that things would be much better if we let
the Thunderbirds go hayriding on their own. To the bewilder-
ment of our counselors, who had no way of forcing us to accept

a treat, all of the campers, gently but immovably, refused to go.

After dinner, Ellen, Chen-cheu, and I, and the other girls from our tent, took part in a desultory sunset game of Capture the Flag as the Thunderbirds and their girls, escorted by Grayfeather staff members, boarded the wagon. An hour and a half later, the returning wagon creaked slowly up to the rec hall. Norah Pfleisch, a plump, excitable junior counselor, rushed inside and burst into tears on the shoulder of Ned Woolworth's wife, Hannah, who was directing a spur-of-the-moment Ping-Pong tournament.

"I've never, *never* had anything like this happen," sobbed Norah, resisting Hannah's efforts to lead her out of the rec hall and away from the fascinated gaze of forty campers. "They— fornicated! They lay in the hay like animals and just . . . did it! It started when we went under the old covered bridge. It was such a beautiful night. Usually we *sing* on hayrides, but this time I didn't know *where* to look, or *what* to listen to!"

We all rushed to the door of the rec hall. Outside, under a clear night sky streaked with meteor showers, the Thunderbirds and their girls, chattering loudly and innocently, were climbing out of the wagon, pulling hay out of each others' clothes.

Things fell apart completely the next day. That morning at swimming class another fight broke out, this one between Femi, the camper from Nigeria, and an agile, pale-skinned, sullen-faced Thunderbird. On the shore in front of the swimming area of the lake, as the white rope and bright floats of the lane dividers bobbed gaily in the morning sun, two counselors held back the two struggling boys in bathing suits, Femi with a swollen nostril leaking blood. "I'll kill that filthy little nigger bastard," panted Femi in his Mayfair accent, wiping his nose with his coal-black arm. "I'll smear his dirty little arse all over the beach. He called me a monkey!"

"He spit on me," the Thunderbird was muttering, scuffling his feet in the sand. "Motherfucker spit on me."

Marvin Jones was called over to make peace. "This ain't no way to act," he began, but his tone was insincere, the tone of a showman bent on pleasing everyone. He sent a quick, shifty grin over to the Thunderbirds standing near him, and one of them suddenly shoved a camper, who went sprawling into the lake. In the boys' swim group a general melee broke out between campers and Thunderbirds, the tanned bodies of the campers mingling wildly with the small, dark, muscular Thunderbirds. The two counselors were themselves dragged in. Pairs of boys bolted, yelling threats, and ran off into the woods.

The girls at the lake, both Thunderbirds and campers, were quickly marched off to our tents, where we were told to sit quietly. Back at her trunk, Chen-cheu looked and found that someone had taken three of her prettiest t-shirts and a new bathing suit. When she complained loudly about it, she found herself surrounded by three Thunderbird girls, including our tentmate Belinda. They began to jostle Chen-cheu and to pluck at her long black hair; Chen-cheu promptly socked Belinda in the stomach. Our counselor Molly came running down the path from the rec hall at precisely the moment when Chen-cheu, propelled by a nasty push, came flying out of the tent to sprawl in the dust and shriek out a string of curses that even Ellen and I had never heard her use. Her beautiful face was contorted and almost purple with rage, but she wasn't crying. None of us were. After that we were separated from the Thunderbird girls.

Meanwhile, the boys were being rounded up. I heard later that a number of them were found grappling in twos and threes in the woods; there were surprisingly few injuries beyond a few black eyes and bloody noses. "We had a plan," one of the boy campers said afterward. "We were going to barricade ourselves in the infirmary and fight 'em off from there. Firebomb them."

The Thunderbird boys, escorted by several strapping counselors called in from a tennis camp across the lake, were confined to the rec hall. By eleven o'clock on a fine, sharp, hot August morning, Camp Grayfeather had settled into a stillness in which the only sounds were those of a sublimely untroubled nature—birdsong; the harsh whirring of cicadas; the light slapping of waves on the lake shore.

None of us was surprised to discover that the Thunderbirds were to be sent home. I sat with nine other girls on the sagging bunks of our tent as Hannah Woolworth, her plump, kindly face pale and drawn with strain beneath its sunburn and freckles, talked to us. "We all feel that it would be better and safer for everyone," she said. "We don't want any of you kids getting hurt."

When she said "you kids," it was clear that she did not mean the Thunderbirds.

I looked at Ellen and Chen-cheu, and they looked back at me. Events were passing, as usual, into the unreachable sphere of adult justice, and though there was a certain relief in that, it also seemed sad. For a day and a half, the Thunderbirds, like a small natural disaster, had given an edge of crazy danger to life at Grayfeather; now the same powers that had brought them to us were taking them away.

"We didn't even get a chance to learn all their names," said Ellen slowly, after Hannah Woolworth had left.

A flicker of resentment ran through the group of girls crowded together in the tent, and Ellen and I began, with an obscure feeling of defiance, to teach the others the song that the Thunderbirds had sung for us under the oak tree the day before.

In about two hours, after we'd eaten a large pile of bologna sandwiches on horrid white bread, sandwiches that the camp cook had provided as a sort of emergency take-out lunch, we heard through the woods the unmistakable sound of a bus. "We've *got* to see this," I said.

Five of us—Ellen, Chen-cheu and I, and two other girls—jumped up and, against the strict instructions left us by our absent counselor, took off toward the rec hall. We didn't take the path but ran dodging like Indian spies through the underbrush, stifling occasional nervous giggles and trying to avoid the poison ivy. When we got to the edge of the clearing, we stood discreetly back in the bushes and observed the scene. The midday sun gave the clearing a close, sleepy feeling. The Thunderbirds, their spirits apparently undaunted, stood in a rambunctious platoon behind a grim-faced Ned Woolworth, and the familiar graffiti-covered school bus was just coming to a halt in the parking lot.

We could see that the same tall, curly-haired man who had delivered the Thunderbirds was coming to pick them up; this time he was wearing a green eyeshade, as if he'd been interrupted during a stretch of desk work. He came quickly down the bus steps and strode over to stand in front of the assembled Thunderbirds. "Well," he said, clapping his hands together, "what the hell have you guys been doing *now?*"

The Thunderbirds, all of them, broke into loud laughter, as if he had just told them the best joke in the world.

"We ain't been doing *nothing,* man," answered Marvin Jones, rocking on his heels. "Just being ourselves!"

The curly-haired man pulled off his visor and sighed so that even we could hear him, fixing his weary, skeptical gaze for a second on Marvin Jones's scarred face, and then on the golden hills and fields of the Delaware countryside rolling into the distance. He talked to Ned Woolworth in a low voice for a few minutes and then turned back to his charges and sighed again. "Come on, get on the bus. We're going back to the city," was all he said to the Thunderbirds.

When we five girls heard the bus start up, we did something we hadn't planned to do. Without any one of us suggesting it, we all took to our heels again and ran through the woods to a dusty crossroads far from the clearing, a spot we knew the bus had to pass. Through some extraordinary, even magical, coincidence the same plan had occurred to all of us. When the bus came rattling up to the crossroads a few seconds after we got there, the five of us, like guerrilla fighters, dashed out of the bushes onto the road. "Stop the bus! Stop for a minute!" we shouted.

The bus slowed and halted, with a squeal of gears, and the Thunderbirds stuck their heads out of the windows. We could see Marvin Jones's platinum streak shining beside Belinda's patch of dyed red hair. "We wanted to sing your song," said Ellen, and without further ado we all began clapping our hands and chanting the profane verses that belonged to the Thunderbirds. "What the word / Thunderbird . . ."

We probably looked ridiculous—five girls in cutoffs, football t-shirts, and moccasins, clapping and trying to perform like a group of tough guys on a city street corner—but we felt natural, synchronized, as if we were doing a good job. When we had finished, the Thunderbirds—still hanging from the windows of the bus—gave us a burst of grave, polite applause. Marvin Jones leaned farther forward out of the window. "That sounded good," he said. "And we're sorry to leave."

The two groups looked at each other, and it seemed for a minute that some obscure misunderstanding was about to be cleared up. Then the bus started up and moved slowly away through the trees.

# An Old
# Woman

Early one Saturday morning my mother and I had a long, monotonous argument about a nifty pair of French jeans that I wanted to buy at Saks. My mother said that the jeans were overpriced and indecently tight, and that she and my father didn't give me an allowance to have me waste it on any fad that came along; I contended that the jeans were a necessity, that I had fewer pairs than any other girl in the neighborhood, and that she just wanted to keep me badly dressed and looking like a child.

We were driving around doing errands. Mama sat up very straight behind the steering wheel, looking prim and slightly ruthless in a dark-green suit, and I slumped in the seat beside her, biting my nails and tapping the toes of my sneakers with boredom. After stopping in at Saks, we had bought some groceries, picked up some flats of marigolds at Korvettes, dropped in at my orthodontist's office to see about a possible crack in my retainer, and stopped at Mrs. Rindell's house to deliver some tickets Mama was selling for a benefit given by her club, the Wives of Negro Professionals. It was a hot, hazy morning, one of a spell of unseasonably warm September days in Philadelphia. Along City Line Avenue the trees were slowly turning brown, and in the diffused light the big street with its crowded shopping centers and dense streams of traffic looked as if it had been lightly powdered by a fall of yellowish dust—it was the same yellow tint that comes over old Polaroid snapshots.

There was one more errand left to do: my mother indicated a brown bag that held a quarter of a poundcake wrapped in wax paper. "I want to take this over to poor old Mrs. Jeller," she said. "Roosevelt Convalescent Home is only five minutes away, and we can just duck in and say hello, and then we can go home."

"Oh, God, Mom—do I have to go in?" I asked.

"You certainly do," said my mother emphatically. "Mrs. Jeller was one of your father's most faithful parishioners a long time ago—possibly in early Christian days—and it would be a pleasure for her to see you. Sit up straight, and stop gnawing at your thumb."

The convalescent home wasn't five minutes away, it was twenty-five, the amount of time it took to go from the crowded thoroughfare of suburban shopping centers at the edge of town to a run-down, oddly deserted city street lined with boarded-up row houses and brick apartment buildings. The wheels of our car rattled on the cobblestones between the trolley tracks; at one end of the street I saw a group of little girls jumping double-dutch, their thin brown legs flying between the whirling ropes.

Old Mrs. Jeller's room opened off a shiny red linoleum corridor on the eighth floor of a tall, dismal building of pale, graffiti-covered brick. The room was a tiny cubicle half filled by a double bed covered with a yellow satin spread; a big television with the picture on but the sound off flickered in the corner. The air was smotheringly hot and smelled strongly of liniment. When I came with my mother through the doorway, I was embarrassed to see Mrs. Jeller seated bare-legged on the bed, wearing a short, rather tight cotton shift that revealed the shape of her large, limp breasts. The old woman was brown-skinned, with a handsome square face; her loose gray hair bounced in a wild frizzy mass around her shoulders, and she kept tossing it back from her face with a petulant gesture that was like a macabre parody of the way a flirtatious teenager might behave. Her expression, which had been drawn and querulous, brightened somewhat when she saw us.

"Come on in, pastor's wife, and sit down!" she called out to my mother in a voice that seemed over-loud and silly to me. She gestured us toward two rangy oak side chairs that looked as if they had come out of a country parlor. "Me and Miz Bryant was just watching TV."

Mrs. Bryant turned out to be the resident social worker, a white woman of about thirty, wearing an Indian-print dress and with a hairdo of untidy curls over a face with a receding chin and a mild, regretful expression, like that of a sheep. Mama handed her the package for Mrs. Jeller, and then all of us sat down. For a minute or two the old woman stared at Mama and me with bright eyes and an unsmiling mouth, still tossing back her hair with that petulant gesture; then she gave a small chuckle. "I can tell you all is mother and daughter," she said. "They ain't no way you could deny that."

"Is that *your* mother over there in the picture, Mrs. Jeller?" asked my mother, indicating an almost indecipherable yellow daguerreotype of a woman that stood on a table beside the bed.

"Yes, ma'am, it is," said Mrs. Jeller. "But she didn't raise me. I came up the hard way."

She moved laboriously backward on the bed and then stretched out her bare legs on the mattress until they lay stiffly in front of her like a doll's legs. On the other side of the bed, the social worker had turned her mournful sheep's face toward the silent television, where a game-show host, like a genie, conjured up prize after prize for a woman who seemed to be weeping with excitement.

"Oh, dear," began my mother. "What a shame. How—"

"The hard way," repeated Mrs. Jeller, striking the mattress with a loud whack. She flung her bushy hair back impatiently and turned to address me as if we were alone in the room. "How old are you, missy? Fifteen?"

"Sixteen," I muttered, abashed. The sight of this wild old woman with the bare legs and shamelessly tossing breasts both disgusted and fascinated me; seeing her was shocking in a curiously intimate way, like learning a terrifying secret about myself.

Mrs. Jeller sat up a little straighter and went on staring at me. Her gaze was severe, as if she were about to chastise me for something. "You're a pretty thing," she said in a reproving tone, and was silent for a minute, her eyes glittering like two black beads in her dry brown face.

"Do you know, girl," she continued abruptly, "that I had my first man—that a man first had his way with me—when I was twelve years old? *Twelve years old!*"

The old woman drew out these last three words into a plaintive wail that sounded like the voice of an abandoned child. As she spoke, she suddenly turned her head from me and began staring out of the window.

My mother gave a dry little cough and asked, "What town did you grow up in, Mrs. Jeller? Was it Philadelphia?"

Mrs. Jeller shook her head. "No, ma'am. It was out in the back of nowhere in Kentucky. Mama worked for the white folks, so I lived with Uncle Mills and Aunt Treece. They were country folks, and up until I was twelve, they kept me innocent. I was so innocent that when I first got Eve's curse, my monthly flow of blood, I thought I had cut myself in the privy. I came running back to the house, shouting to my uncle and aunt, 'I've hurt myself!'

"Aunt Treece took me upstairs and showed me the cloths I must use to catch the blood, and how I must boil and wash them. And Uncle Mills called me into the parlor and told me that now I was a woman, and from that night on, I must only take my pants down for two reasons—to wash, and to go to the privy.

"Both of them warned me never to allow any men or boys near me. But strict as they could be, a man did get to me. He was the brother of two girls who lived down the road. They were fast girls, bad girls, older than I was; they used to smoke little violet-colored cigarettes. They would always say 'Come on!' to me whenever they went places, and like a fool I'd go. And then their brother took to hanging around, and one night the girls left the two of us alone, and he did something to me. He hurt me, and I didn't even know what it was he was doing. I ran home and didn't stop to speak to my uncle and aunt—I just went right on up to bed and cried. Three weeks later my uncle looked at me and said, 'Honey, you been with a man. Who was it?'

"I started to cry and told him all about it. It turned out that I had gotten a baby from that man, from just that one time. A man's seed is a powerful thing. It wiggles and jumps until it gets where it's going, even inside a child who was a virgin.

"The next morning my uncle went out, and when he came back, he said to me, 'Hattie, we are going to have a wedding here, so go and invite whoever you want.'

"I invited my teacher from school, and a girl I played with from next door, and I stood in the parlor, and the preacher married me to that man—his name was John. And after that, John lived in our house, and slept in my room, though I hardly spoke to him. Oh, it was frightening, I tell you, to wake up with that strange head alongside of me on the pillow. One night he touched me, and I felt a leaping and a hopping inside of me, as if my baby was trying to come out. After that I wouldn't let him touch me. And in June, when my baby came, my uncle had the marriage annulled."

Mrs. Jeller shivered suddenly and clasped her hands with a sudden movement that shook her limp breasts under the cotton shift. "I can't seem to get warm, even on hot days," she said. "I can't even sleep with regular sheets now," she continued, indicating the bed, which was made up with a pair of thin, stained cotton blankets. Through the window came the hazy September sunlight, and from the street below, faintly, drifted the shouts of children and the noise of passing cars.

My mother and I both had our eyes fixed on the old woman as if we were hypnotized. "What happened to your baby?" I asked, almost involuntarily.

Mrs. Jeller looked off toward Mrs. Bryant, the social worker, who was still watching the silent television. "For a year and a half, my baby lived," she said. "It was a baby girl. I left school and went out to work for white folks, and my lady, Miz Guthrie, was crazy about my baby. 'Little Daisy,' she named her, and kept her in a big basket in the dining room. She called me every hour to nurse the baby. That child saw more white society than I ever did. But she sickened and died; a lot of children died in those days. Two years later I was fourteen and free of husband and daughter. Free of both of them, and still a child myself."

The old woman suddenly turned her head back toward Mama and me, and gave us a toothless smile so wide and so swift that it seemed demonic. We both rose abruptly from our chairs as if we'd been struck from behind. Once on my feet, I really felt as if I might faint from the stifling heat of the room and the smell of liniment.

"It's been very nice to see you," said my mother, after making a bit of small talk.

"Nicer for me than for you," said Mrs. Jeller, with a wink.

When we stood waiting for the elevator in the red linoleum hallway of the nursing home, I felt unwilling to look my mother in the face, and she seemed disinclined to look at me. We stood awkwardly, half facing away from each other, and I felt very aware of my body under my clothes. For the first time, I was sensing the complicated possibilities of my own flesh—possibilities of corruption, confused pleasure, even death. The tale we'd heard—that had burst so unexpectedly upon a dullish Saturday afternoon—had a disturbing archaic flavor; it seemed, even, in a vague way, obscene. In its light it was hard for us to face each other as mother and child. We had not yet arrived at an acquaintance with each other as two women, and so we had to remain silent.

"I never heard *that* story before," said Mama finally, taking a handkerchief from her purse and patting the sides of her neck. "Poor old thing, she's gotten very senile."

"It was awfully hot in there," I said, gathering up my hair in my hands and flapping it to make a breeze.

"Old people like hot rooms. Their limbs don't seem to hold any warmth."

We got in the car and began the long drive back to the suburbs, and after a minute or two it was possible to talk naturally. We never, however, resumed our formulaic argument over the French jeans: one visible effect of our visit to old Mrs. Jeller was that ever afterward I was allowed to pick out my own clothes. My mother explained it by saying that she guessed I was old enough to make any mistake I chose.

# Negatives

I hadn't exactly grown up with Curry Daniels, but almost—he was even kind of related. Our mothers were distant cousins and had been best friends at Philadelphia Girls' High School; side by side, wearing floppy, Depression-style hats, they had trilled sedately through endless Sunday afternoons in the Young Women's Choir of the New African Baptist Church. Throughout my childhood my mother received a couple of Daniels family snapshots every few months, sent in letters from Atlanta, where Curry's family had moved after the Second World War, and where his father had become a county supervisor. From the photographs, and from two visits to Atlanta, I knew that Curry (whose real name was John Curbin) lived in the same kind of surroundings I did in Philadelphia: a comfortable, insular, middle-class black neighborhood swathed in billiard-green lawns.

Once, when I was very small, Curry and his two younger brothers visited Philadelphia, and the band of little boys—they had gathered in Matthew—harried me cruelly, unbraiding my plaits and threatening me with homemade blowpipes and twigs they said were baby rattlers. Much later, when I was in ninth grade, a snapshot of a rangy adolescent Curry (he was two years older than I was) with his legs negligently sprawled in the back seat of a Mustang convertible kept me awake and restless through a few starry May nights. After a while, though, I thought

about him only when I had to send Christmas thank-you notes
to his family.

When I left home in the early nineteen-seventies to go to
Harvard, Mama gave me Curry's number at Winthrop House
and instructed me to call him, but of course I didn't. I'd almost
forgotten he was at the same school until I saw him one cold
December morning in a lecture on *King Lear.* After class I ran
down the steep steps of the lecture hall and caught Curry as he
was stepping out onto Cambridge Street. It was snowing, and he
was wearing a big down jacket; when I gave him a sudden timid
squeeze, the puffs of down collapsed softly, as if he were melting
away in my embrace. "Sarah! You've certainly turned into a
fascinating stranger!" he said, staring at me and grinning, and
I felt a happy little flutter in my throat.

I thought *he* looked pretty much the same as always—a bit like
me, in fact, with his lean face that showed an almost evenly
balanced mixture of black, white, and Indian blood. Below a
mass of dark curls that he had tried, vainly, to shape into an Afro,
his forehead was very high and bulgy, giving him a whiz-kid look
of precocious intelligence, and his eyes, which were small,
greenish, and very bright, peered through a pair of old-fashioned gold-rimmed spectacles that made him resemble, at times,
an earnest young yeshiva scholar. His mouth was prettily shaped
and rather pursed, the mouth of a spoiled boy. Under his jacket
he was wearing jeans, a blue flannel shirt, and, draped rather
dramatically around his neck, a Moroccan scarf; over one shoulder he carried a Pentax camera.

After this first meeting Curry and I became friends. We often
discussed whether or not this was proper: it was a friendship that
would give great pleasure to both of our families, and that was
something that neither of us particularly wanted to do. During
the fall and winter of my sophomore year we wasted dozens of
afternoons together over cooling cups of coffee in the Winthrop
House dining room. Sometimes we played repetitive games, like
trying to flip a cigarette butt into a glass across the table; other
times we talked about a scholarly circle we'd invented that re-
volved around an imaginary publication called *Condiment Review.*
"Have you seen Spazzola's monograph 'Restructuring Relish'?
Absurd. The price of dillweed alone . . ."

We thought we were awfully clever. Curry was a visual studies
major who was planning—with the insouciance that returned so
suddenly to male students after the end of the Vietnam draft—

to spend a year after his graduation that June traveling and
taking pictures in northern Brazil. I was concentrating in English and putting the finishing touches on a collection of angu-
lar-looking poems with a lot of asterisks in them. Like most of
our friends, Curry and I both harbored ill-conceived ideals of
leading lives that would almost geometrically contravene anything of which our parents would approve. We spent a lot of
time talking about what it meant to come from the kind of
earnest, prosperous black family in which civil rights and con-
cern for the underprivileged are served up, so to speak, at breakfast, lunch, and dinner. "It made us naughty and perverse,"
insisted Curry. When he was home on vacation, he liked to
scandalize his father, veteran of a score of nonviolent desegrega-
tion campaigns, with long quotations from Marcuse and Che
Guevara.

The funny thing was that when I was with Curry, as daringly
as we talked, I didn't feel much like the anarchistic poet I hoped
I might be. When I was with him, in fact, I experienced a sweet
feeling of nostalgia, a faint but concentrated and lingering suggestion of dear past days in the small world of home and family.

Encountering Curry at Harvard had reawakened a memory I
hadn't been aware of for many years: it was an image of a Sunday
morning in autumn, during the time his family had visited our
house in Philadelphia. Very early—before the grownups had
come downstairs, and while Curry's two little brothers were still
asleep—Curry, Matthew, and I, all of us in pajamas, had been
on our knees on the dining-room rug, reading the comics. The
first sunlight was shining through reddish leaves and gauze curtains at the window, striking the polished legs of the furniture
around us, and over everything lay the magical freshness and
conspiratorial quiet of the awakening day. As I pored over the
bright-colored funny paper, my brother made a rather labored
joke (I thought) about the comics being full of "nuts"—"nut"
being a derisive nickname the boys had bestowed on me. Curry
looked at me and gave a cruel snicker; as he did so, a sunbeam
struck his round cheek, and I saw for the first time, with the
feeling of having learned a secret, that at the corner of his left
eye he had a birthmark shaped like a long tear. It was faint, but
it lay on his cheek with a formal precision, like the stylized tears
clowns sometimes paint on their faces.

I never mentioned the birthmark to him, not even when I met
him again in college, but my eyes automatically sought it out as

something reassuring, a familiar landmark, whenever I sat down to have lunch with him in the Winthrop House dining room. Sometimes we lingered so long that they turned out the lights on us; in the early dusk of fall and winter the dim, high-ceilinged room seemed like a cave. We usually sat at one of the side tables, two little figures dwarfed by the tall, many-paned windows, cracking jokes and guffawing as the kitchen help walked back and forth in the half-light. Occasionally the stout Irishwomen who served the meals would give us curious glances that we imagined were hostile—it was a year of accelerating race conflict in South Boston—and Curry responded by talking in an outrageous Georgia redneck accent that he'd learned at his fancy prep school.

On Wednesdays Curry's girlfriend Philippa would join us after her tutorial. Philippa was a blonde from New York, undeniably beautiful, but a little faded and monotone in coloring, a fine-arts major with feminist ideas that she expressed in an incongruous wispy, little girl's voice. She and I professed warm friendship, but I made fun of her behind her back. "Phil's like an aquatint of Gloria Steinem," I once remarked to Curry, and he, disloyally, agreed.

Curry and I used up a lot of energy making fun of each other's lovers; each of us treated the other's romantic escapades as if they were recurring bouts of insanity. Curry was especially cruel about a Chinese law student I went out with for a few weeks during my sophomore year. "Why don't you go out with your own kind, dear?" he asked me one afternoon in a meddlesome, grandmotherly manner. "Your circle of men is like the United Nations."

"Look who's talking," I snapped back. "You'd better find a black girlfriend before you get yourself thrown out of that Frantz Fanon study group."

"You and I ought to get married," said Curry, abstractedly twiddling his bony fingers. "Except with such a nice colored girl and a nice colored boy, it would be . . ."

"A little too boring," I finished for him.

With girls of any color, Curry was popular. He was the most successful kind of flirt, the kind who really knows about women's clothes, and who can look attentive through long monologues about emotions. He was also a wonderful photographer, and that was another way he attracted girls: he took arty portrait shots that became quite the thing in some circles at Harvard. In his pictures pretty girls perched in fey poses in the branches of trees in Radcliffe Yard or, in trailing Indian dresses, lounged against tombstones in Christ Church cemetery. Sometimes he photographed them nude, with contemplative expressions on their faces as they crouched inside cardboard boxes or huddled among heaps of crumpled newspaper. He was so successful at all this that he had already published several pictures—notably "Monica with Onionskin"—in photography magazines, and his telephone line (much to the envy of his suitemates, and to the studied indifference of Philippa) was murmurous with female voices.

Curry had been asking for a long time to do a portrait of me, but I just laughed at him. "You're the last person I'd let take my picture," I told him. "You know too much."

I enjoyed his pictures, however, and I liked to sit and discuss with him the faces and figures of the girls he photographed. (He talked about girls in an abstruse intellectual manner that broke down sometimes into a fraternity-style appraisal of measurements.) And I liked to visit him in the darkroom at Carpenter Center for Visual Arts, where his curly head and intent, spoiled-boy's face glowed through the red darkness, and in the intimate smell of chemicals we watched the developing pictures rise out of the paper.

One afternoon in mid-April of my sophomore year, Curry and I were sitting around in the living room of his suite, waiting for Philippa to arrive so that we could all go down for an early dinner. (It was roast-beef-and-ice-cream night at Winthrop House.) Half an hour before, we'd had a beer with Curry's suitemate Grant, a burned-out surfer from a rich family that seemed to own half of Honolulu. (I often thought that the three suitemates, Grant, Curry, and Ted—a shy black work-study student from the Mississippi Delta—formed an interesting social continuum.) Talking to suntanned Grant, who found it hard to put three sentences together without using the words "bummer" or "dynamite weed," had depressed me; after he left to sleep in the library, I sat dispiritedly on the sagging twin bed that served as a couch, looking at a contact sheet of pictures Curry had taken of Philippa during a weekend on Nantucket.

"She looks fantastic here," I said to Curry, who was sitting cross-legged in a big red leather chair that had yellowish stuffing showing through a dozen tears and slashes. "Ten times more alive than in real life. How did you do it?"

"That's an incredibly nasty thing to say, but I know what you mean. Sometimes she works better for me on film."

He had been splicing together one of his obscure blues tapes —it was typical of Curry to be pedantic about music, and meticulous in the upkeep of his elaborate stereo system—but suddenly, in one agile movement, he laid down the tape and swung his skinny legs to the floor. "Come on, Sarah, let me take your picture. Right now. You haven't been thinking about it, so you'll be natural."

"But Phil's coming for dinner."

"That won't make any difference. She's cool. She watches me shoot all the time. Come on, there's enough light. I'll set up the tripod."

"Do you want me to take off my clothes?"

For less than a second—one of the infinitesimal fragments of time that determine how a remark is given or received—Curry hesitated. Then he said, in his normal relaxed, teasing voice: "Well, I think that's the best thing you can do. We can roll you up in Grant's tapa cloth, or have you climbing the bookcases, or something. We might get some fantastic shots."

I went into Curry's bedroom and pushed the door three-quarters closed. It seemed stupid to be modest about the act of undressing when I was willing to prance around naked in front of a camera; I was surprised to find, however, that I was deeply unwilling to have Curry see me in the graceless process of disrobing: legs stuck in my jeans and underwear, head lost in my sweater. When I had pulled off my clothes, I tossed them onto Curry's bed, a big double mattress he and Philippa had bought from the Salvation Army. It lay on the floor, almost filling the tiny room, covered with rumpled sheets and bearing on one pillow an ashtray full of dried-out apple cores. Over the desk and the crammed bookshelf beside the bed were taped photographs and contact sheets, as well as three posters that showed Curry's eccentric range of interests: a black and red notice for a Caribbean Marxist rally, a poster from a psychedelic minimalist exhibition that depicted what looked like a radioactive pea, and an enlarged reproduction of a Burne-Jones angel.

From outside the window came the sleepy mumbling of a pigeon that had somehow managed to land there despite the anti-pigeon spikes on the outer sill. I could see part of a brick wall, and a few bits of ivy flapping in the breeze. The suite was overheated as usual, and it felt good to be out of my clothes. I looked down at my body, which I knew was pretty, and felt a frisky excitement in being able to show it off to Curry. It was strange, I thought, that we had never seen each other naked before: at that time the groups of friends we both went around with found constant excuses to have chaste, tingly nude encounters, all organized in the name of a specious artistic freedom.

When I came out of the bedroom, I called mockingly, "Get ready for the thrill of your life!"

Curry had been adjusting the height of the tripod. When he looked up, there was another of those minute, crucial pauses. Then he said, in a dry voice, "How perfect you are."

In a minute we managed to adopt the intimate, jocular tone we normally used with each other, and the picture-taking session went forward at a smart pace. Curry urged me to do things with my hands or chin, or to "approach and react to the couch," in a pretentious, slightly British accent he had clearly picked up from watching David Hemmings in *Blow-Up*. The poses we tried were amusing or acrobatic rather than erotic: neither of us quite knew what to do with my naked body. When Philippa finally came in, pushing her long hair out of her face, smiling with her usual air of thin-blooded pleasure at seeing me, and looking unsurprised to find me crouching bare as a newt on top of the couch, I was glad enough to go back into the untidy bedroom and put my clothes on.

A couple of days later, in the Carpenter Center darkroom, Curry developed the rolls of film he had shot of me, and I came along to see the results. The pictures were all horrible. After my first shriek I was able to observe, objectively, that while the body of the girl in the photographs looked relaxed and normal, her face was subtly distorted and her neck strained, as if an invisible halter were dragging her backward.

"You were pretty nervous," said Curry, clipping one enlargement up on a drying rack.

I looked at him, and he looked at me. We were very close together, closer than when our knees bumped occasionally under the dining tables at Winthrop House. In the red light his gold-rimmed glasses gleamed rosily, and his green plaid shirt looked black. The open neck of the shirt showed the tender-looking skin that stretched over his knobby collarbones, and for the first time since I had known him, with what was less a conscious thought than an impulse of my flesh, I was curious about how it would feel to touch his throat, his chest. At the same time

I wondered briefly and coldly why Curry and I had never become lovers. The answer was fairly clear, as we stared at each
other with eyes almost alike enough to be those of siblings, into
faces that for each of us symbolized the unbearably familiar
things of life.

Curry began to laugh and waved a handful of negatives under
my nose. "I'll sell 'em to you," he said. "Let me have five thousand in unmarked bills, or prints go straight to your parents."
As he spoke, he was stuffing negatives, contact sheets, and two
dry prints he had enlarged earlier into a manila envelope.
"Here," he said, handing it to me.

"I don't want these."

"Take them anyway." He had stopped laughing and spoke in
a sharper voice than he had ever used with me before; and,
unaccountably, I felt tears start to my eyes. I took the envelope
quickly, looking away from him.

We talked studiously about movies as we came out of the
darkroom and walked up the gray driveway of Carpenter Center,
and slowly I began to feel a lot better—relieved, as if an obscure
crisis had passed. Across Kirkland Street the Memorial Church
bell was ringing six o'clock. It had been a beautiful day, warmer
than usual for April in Boston, and a yellow-green haze of budding trees hung over Harvard Yard. Kids were lounging on the
steps of the libraries to catch the last of the waning sun, and
Frisbee players shouted and leaped on the grass around the
freshmen houses. In a single sunny afternoon the miracle had
occurred that always galvanizes college campuses: summer, the
shining irresponsible season that lies beyond the barrier of term
papers and exams, had come into view.

I shifted my knapsack on my shoulders and reflected that
summer meant commencement for Curry, who would then take
off on his peculiar pilgrimage to eat *feijoada* among the Bahians,
or whatever he intended to do. For me the summer meant the
beginning of a time without my friend. This was something I
thought of unhappily, but without tremendous perturbation,
because I had the feeling that no matter what happened, I would
always be running into Curry—that our particular bond of fascination and repulsion would bounce us together to resume,
again and again, a dialogue that would always seem familiar, but
never dull.

We walked through the Yard and paused at one of the gate-
ways, where a friend of mine, a tall Jamaican kid named Hunter,

was passing out leaflets praising revolutionary activity in the Third World. Across the street nine Hare Krishnas, looking uncharacteristically buoyant and chipper in the bright spring evening, were hopping and chanting in front of the Harvard Coop. Curry had to go: Philippa was taking him to see *Yojimbo*, and I had to camp out in the library to finish an overdue paper on Yeats. When I had said goodbye and started walking up toward the Radcliffe dorms, I heard footsteps behind me and turned around to find Curry, out of breath from the run.

"Hey, please don't throw away those pictures!" he said, taking off his glasses, which had gotten fogged up with perspiration, and raking his fingers through his dark curls, which were standing up even more wildly than usual. With his glasses off, his little tear-shaped birthmark was clearly visible, and the sight of it was enough to dissolve any trace of the strange irritation and grief I had felt in the darkroom. "At least hang on to the negatives," he went on. "Maybe I can try to shoot you again. I'd like to have something to work with."

I promised him I would keep everything—but, in fact, at the first trash can I came to, on Garden Street, I had a change of heart and tossed in the manila envelope, negatives and all. When we were hanging out together in the next few weeks, I was afraid, once or twice, that he might try to get the pictures back from me, but he never mentioned them again.

That summer, after Curry had graduated and I had come home to Philadelphia for two months, my mother, with the indiscreet eagerness that sometimes overwhelms even tactful parents, asked if there was "anything romantic" between Curry and me.

"Not a chance," I said.

"There are chances for all kinds of things," she said coyly.

"Not for that." At that point I didn't feel sure of much in my life, but for once I felt I had said something that was absolutely true.

# Fine Points

One great thing about Margaret was that she wore exactly the same size clothing that I did, an excellent quality in a roommate; she had, however, completely different taste, with an inclination toward plunging necklines, crimson tights, and minidresses in big, bold Scandinavian prints. My own wardrobe ran to jeans and black turtlenecks, odd little somber-colored tunics that I felt made me look like a wood nymph, and short pleated skirts that seemed to me to convey a sexy *jeune fille* air worthy of Claudine at school. "You literary types are always trying to look understated," Margaret would say whenever she saw me dressed for seminar, for an *Advocate* meeting, or for a date. She was a chemistry major from Wellesley, Massachusetts, an avid lacrosse player with a terrific figure and a pair of unabashed blue eyes that revealed a forceful, stubborn nature—Margaret could keep an argument going for days. She adored fresh air and loathed reticence and ambiguity, and she had little patience with a roommate who, languid from lack of exercise, spent weeks reworking a four-word line of poetry.

"It's a question of fine points," I would retort loftily, though I had only a vague idea of what that might mean.

Margaret and I got along well for young women with such different souls. We spent a lot of time together in our cramped dormitory suite, squabbling comfortably over clothes and discussing romance—the one subject on which we were, to some extent, in agreement. The suite was on the fourth floor of Currier House; it consisted of two tiny rooms, a bathroom we'd decorated for a giggle with pinups of the bustiest *Playboy* Playmates we could find, and a kitchenette filled with moldy oranges stolen from the cafeteria. Our windows faced east, toward the corner of Garden and Linnaean streets—a lovely view, really, with the Observatory woods, the flat-bottomed, whale-shaped clouds that came sailing down from Maine, and the tall, somber Cambridge houses back of the trees.

In the winter of 1973, our junior year at Harvard, on afternoons when Margaret was back from the lab and I was supposed to be at my desk reading Donne and Herbert for seminar or writing poetry for Professor Hawks's versification class, we would hang out in Margaret's room and drink oolong tea, which Margaret brewed so black it became a kind of solvent. Lounging on Margaret's bed, below a periodic table she'd tacked up on the wall, we'd complain at length about our boyfriends. These young men, a couple of blameless seniors from Adams and Dunster Houses, were certainly ardent and attentive, but they bored us because they seemed appropriate. We yearned, in concert, to replace them with unsuitable men—an array of Gothic-novel types who didn't seem at all hackneyed to Margaret and me. (Margaret, the scientist, had in fact a positively Brontëesque conception of the ideal man.) We envisioned liaisons with millionaires the age of our fathers, with alcoholic journalists, with moody filmmakers addicted to uppers; Margaret's particular thing was depraved European nobility. A few years earlier it might have been possible for me to find the necessary thrill simply in going out with white boys, the forbidden fruit of my mother's generation; but in the arty circles I frequented at Harvard, such pairings were just about required, if one was to cut any dash at all.

What our fantasies boiled down to was that Margaret and I, in the age-old female student tradition, ended up angling for members of the faculty.

"It's just a question of days before Dr. Bellemere tumbles," said Margaret one afternoon. (She flirted shamelessly with her adviser, but for some reason could not bring herself to call him by his first name—Don.) "And *then,* what naughty delights!"

As a matter of fact, I was the one who first was offered the chance to taste those delights. In February a genuine instructor —Geoffrey Knacker, who had taught my seminar on metaphysical poetry the previous semester, and who shared an apartment in Central Square with Millicent Tunney, another junior faculty member—asked me to meet him for a cup of coffee. Margaret sat cross-legged on my bed while I got dressed for the date— we were to meet at six at the Café Pamplona—and grew snappish when I refused the loan of a pair of red tights. She told me that if I hid my light under a bushel, I wouldn't even get him to kiss me. I didn't listen to her. I was busy making myself look as beautiful and mysterious as I could, and when I had slicked my hair back into a bun, rimmed my eyes with dark pencil, and put on a severe gray dress with a pair of black high heels I had bought in a thrift shop, even Margaret had to applaud the result.

"If Hopalong calls, tell him I'm riding in the Tour de France," I said. Hopalong Cassidy was the name we had privately given my boyfriend, who had what I thought was an unnecessarily jaunty gait.

"You're a cold, hard thing," said Margaret in an approving tone.

I owned a rather rubbed-looking sealskin jacket that had belonged to my mother; when I had wrapped it around me, waved goodbye to the girl who stood studying behind the bells desk of the dormitory, and stepped outside into the February twilight, I had an agreeable feeling of satisfaction about the way I looked, and an agitated romantic feeling about the meeting to come. "Perhaps I'm in love," I thought, though in fact I could barely remember what Geoffrey Knacker looked like.

It was ten minutes to six. I walked down Garden Street toward Cambridge Common, listening to the unaccustomed click of my high heels on the brick sidewalk, slippery with melted snow and patches of dirty ice. In the darkness around me, students riding bicycles or walking with book bags were returning to dinner from classes in Harvard Yard. The sky over the dark buildings and narrow streets was a deep lustrous blue, streaked at the edges with pinkish light, and the air was cold and damp. Near Follen Street a small battered Datsun was trying unsuccessfully to park between a jacked-up Riviera and a Volvo plastered with psychedelic stickers. The sound of grinding gears made me think of the time during my sophomore year when a precursor of my boyfriend Hopalong had gotten very stoned at the Dartmouth game and had pursued me along Garden Street by backing up his car for a whole block, all the while declaiming the words from the Temptations' song "My Girl." The incident had infuriated me at the time, but now I thought of it as something gay and romantic, the sort of thing that happened constantly to a woman destined to exercise a fatal influence upon men.

My feeling of agitation increased as I approached the Common. The usual shouts and guffaws were coming from the war monument in the middle, where Cambridge townies liked to hang around smoking dope and drinking wine, but they seemed far away. I looked through the rows of leafless maples at the university towers and traffic lights clustering ahead of me, and felt an unreasonable, blissful happiness to be walking in high heels and a fur coat on a clear evening to a meeting with a man who was likely to mean trouble—the kind of trouble that mothers and magazine articles particularly warned against. I felt a bit like Anna Karenina, burning with a sinful glow; and as if someone beside me in the darkness had spoken a few passionate, muted words, it seemed to me that I was ravishingly beautiful. I began to pretend that someone *was* walking with me: a lover who didn't resemble my boyfriend, or even Geoffrey Knacker. This imaginary lover, in fact, didn't have much of any appearance at all, only a compelling simplicity of character that granted every dangerous wish I had ever had. As I walked through the Common, giving a wide berth to the monument, where two long-haired girls were giggling beside a guy who looked like Jimi Hendrix, I crooked my fingers very slightly inside the pocket of my fur jacket, as if I were holding hands with someone. And then I did something I never afterward admitted to anyone, not even Margaret: I recited a poem to my invisible companion—Donne's "The Flea."

By the time I got to the Pamplona, I had almost forgotten Geoffrey Knacker, who rose from his tiny table to greet me, with an air of being slightly startled by my appearance. He was a tall, thin man with a mournful, rather handsome face and gray half-moons of skin under his eyes; in the white-tiled, low-ceilinged interior of the Pamplona, surrounded by graduate students chatting over cappuccino, he appeared curiously yellowish and misanthropic, as if he'd lived most of his life in a remote tropical outpost. He helped me with my coat, and I ordered an ice cream. Then the two of us began to talk, rather constrainedly, about metaphysical poetry until Geoffrey began paying me heavy-handed compliments.

"I always felt that behind your reserved manner in class was a rare sensitivity of nature," he said, giving me a slow, gloomy smile, and I, who had been attracted by just that smile in the seminar, found myself filled not with rapture but with an inexplicable annoyance. It occurred to me that this meeting was just like a coffee date with any callow comp lit major, who would begin by throwing out portentous hints about his ideal woman and end, ritually, by suggesting we drop mescaline and swim nude in the Adams House pool. I tried to think of the romantic fact that Geoffrey Knacker was an instructor, and that both of us were flouting lovers in order to meet, but all I could seem to feel was irritation at a flat, straw-colored mole that Geoffrey had where his jaw met his neck, and at the way that as he talked, he joined the tips of his fingers together and pumped them in and out in a tiny bellowslike motion. We were sitting at an inconspicuous table in a corner, but it seemed to me, in my hypersensitive state, that all the other students in the Pamplona could see the mole and the working fingertips, and were laughing discreetly at them.

As I rattled my spoon in my ice-cream dish, some demon prompted me to say, "But certainly you must have seen hundreds of exceptional students in all your years as a teacher."

"Hundreds?" repeated Geoffrey Knacker in an injured tone. "Why, no. I finished my dissertation three years ago. I am only thirty-one."

We didn't really have much to say to each other. It was clear, in fact, that our initial attraction had become puzzling and abortive, and that this meeting was one of those muted social disasters that can be devastating if one cares. I didn't care much; nor, it seemed, did Geoffrey Knacker. We shook hands and parted outside the Pamplona without even the polite device of mentioning plans to get in touch. When he zipped up his jacket and, with one last unhappy smile, trudged off in his L. L. Bean boots toward Central Square, I clicked off back to Radcliffe in my high heels, feeling positively elated. Geoffrey Knacker, I decided, was a bore, but the *fact* of Geoffrey Knacker was exciting. As I came into Harvard Square and threaded my way through the slush and evening traffic on Massachusetts Avenue, the romantic sensation I'd had while walking through the Common returned to me in full force. I seemed, agreeably, to be taking up the strands of an interrupted idyll, and in my right palm, deep in the pocket of the fur jacket, was the pleasant tickling feeling that denoted the grasp of my imaginary lover.

When I got back to the suite, Margaret was working on a

problem sheet for Chem 105, and her boyfriend—a young man with such an earnest, childlike gaze that we'd nicknamed him Christopher Robin—was seated cross-legged on her bed, using a metal mesh contraption to sift seeds and stems out of an ounce of grass he'd just bought. (One of Margaret's complaints about him was his methodical attitude toward sex and drugs.) "Oo-la-la—very thirties," said Christopher Robin, giving my outfit the old once-over, and then Margaret dragged me into the bathroom.

"Well, what happened?" she demanded, locking the door, turning on both faucets, and settling herself on the sink counter under the enormous bosom of one of the Playmates we'd pinned up. "He must have kissed you—or did you fall into bed together? You're absolutely beaming."

"Knacker was actually kind of a fizzle," I said. "But it was fun anyway."

"Idiot child," said Margaret. "Take off that coat—you've wasted it. I knew you should have worn red stockings."

When I tried to explain myself, she leaned back against the bathroom mirror, closed her eyes, and giggled so that the frame of the mirror shook. "My artistic roommate," she said. "The woman of epiphanies. You're going to kill me with your fine points."

A few weeks later Margaret was dancing to a Stones tape at a party in a converted airplane factory up near MIT when she ran into her adviser, Dr. Bellemere, whom she at last succeeded in calling Don. Bellemere, who was a post-doc a bit older than Geoffrey Knacker, and who fluttered hearts all through the chem labs with his leather vest and Buffalo Bill mustache, had had a lot of the punch, which was a Techie grape-juice concoction laced with acid. He led Margaret out of the strobe lights into a dark corner of the loft, kissed her passionately, and told her he spent every lab session thinking about her legs. A triumph for Margaret—except that she inexplicably discovered a preference for Christopher Robin, and so the thing with Bellemere went no further, except for a bit of embarrassment in lab.

"But there was something really solid there—a kiss, not just daydreams," Margaret told me pointedly when we discussed it later. For a change, we were sitting among the scattered books and papers of my room, while I packed my book bag to go down and visit Hopalong at Adams House.

"I don't think the two situations were so different," I said.

"I'm afraid, sweetheart, that whatever we try to do, in our two different ways, we end up being just a couple of nice girls."

"Oh, I hope not!" said Margaret, flopping backward on the bed. "But anyway," she went on stubbornly after a minute, "a real kiss is better than an imaginary one."

And she thumped her booted feet on my bedspread for emphasis.

I wanted to contradict her, but then I remembered how bullheaded and tenacious Margaret could be in an argument, how tiresomely withholding of her oolong tea and the little English butter biscuits that her mother sent her, and that I loved. In the end I just raised my eyebrows with the air of one to whom has been granted higher knowledge, and kept my mouth shut.

# A Funeral at New African

## 1

When my mother called me at school to tell me that my father had had a stroke, it was hard to understand what she said, because the phone was only half working; it had been ripped out of the wall three weeks earlier by an ex-boyfriend of mine named Kiri, a Norwegian graduate student in physics who occasionally got drunk on aquavit and went into berserker rages of jealousy. With the help of my suitemate, the ever-ingenious Margaret, I had managed to piece the phone wires together so that a sort of communication was possible. Mama's voice came through in a series of gasps embroidered with static, and what she said first sent a dissolving feeling through my bones and then became a part of me that seemed as if it had always been there. The facts were simple: my father had been sitting in his office at the New African Baptist Church, dictating a sermon to his secretary, when he had suddenly fallen back in his chair—a fall that in my imagination took on the controlled backward curve of the thousands of bodies he had baptized. He had been taken to the hospital, and I was to come home immediately.

After I had gingerly hung up the phone, I sat down on the bed and looked around my wreck of a room, which I hadn't

put back together after Kiri had pulled it to pieces and I had
told him finally, inexorably, to get lost. Besides yanking out
the phone, he had torn down my tidy blue regulation dormitory curtains and my favorite poster—a Degas sketch of a black
dancer in a Paris café—and he had put his foot through the
stout wooden seat of a Windsor rocker that had belonged to
my great-aunt Sarah Crenshaw. It was only a few months until
commencement, and it had seemed ridiculous to try to rebuild
a cheery student nest with new posters and a shiny Harvard
rocker from the Coop. I had, in fact, begun to take a macabre
delight in the mangled curtain that swayed spastically in the
drafts of March air; in the splintered chair, where the broken
wood looked new against the old black finish; and in the
dancer, hanging upside-down by a shred of tape, a nasty smile
on his face as he pointed a toe before a group of Belle Époque
bloods. On my desk, scattered among five coffee cups and an
array of wizened apples, were the yellow legal pages that held
the second draft of my senior thesis, "The Literature of Adventure in Nineteenth-Century America." During the last
phone conversation I had had with my father, I had tearfully
complained to him about how badly the thesis was going, and
he had irritated me by asking in a voice that was tired and
vacant of all emotion, "Do you think you can straighten things
out on your own?"

"I don't know," I had snapped back angrily. "It's all a mess."

In a few minutes Margaret came back from the chem labs. She
wheeled her ten-speed bicycle into the hallway of the little suite
and threw down her book bag, looking wan and disheveled from
an evening spent poring over enzymes and fatty acids. When I
told her what had happened, she looked at me silently for a
minute, her blue eyes brilliant and wide. Still without saying
anything, she pulled off her big Mexican sweater and turned on
the hot-plate under the teakettle. She brewed a pot of Twinings
Gunpowder Green, bitter and strong enough to take the skin off
the insides of our mouths; we took the tea, a couple of mugs, and
a bottle of Barbadian rum that had been gathering dust on
Margaret's bookshelf and went out onto the balcony of the suite.
We sat down on the edge of the balcony, sticking our legs
through the railing so that they hung down in the darkness over
Linnaean Street. It was about midnight on the Tuesday of a

March week in which the weather had been warm and chaotic—
sudden rains, wet winds, and languorous afternoons so sunny
that Cambridge townies hung out smoking weed in the Common as if it were already May.

That night low clouds were passing on a brownish sky, and the
two of us sat swinging our legs and peering through the leafless
trees at a set of brick faculty apartments behind the dorm. We
sipped the rum and bitter tea and gossiped about our friends
and boyfriends and ex-boyfriends—especially the obnoxious
Kiri—and about what we were going to do after commencement. Margaret was going to take six months off to travel
through the Yucatán with some friends who owned a beat-up
VW camper, and then she was going to go to grad school in
chemistry at Penn. I had made no plans at all, except to write
away halfheartedly, back in September, to a couple of European
universities. All year, until that night, I had found it hard to
believe that I would be leaving college, but there on the balcony
after the phone call about my father, I had a small, gradual but
continuous sensation of removal, as if filament after filament of
the ties that had bound me to my previous life of school and
family were breaking. Since I had spoken to my mother, a tremendous calm had taken possession of me; I saw clearly, as if
at a great distance, that this hour marked a change in everything,
as inconspicuous and profound as the change a tincturing drop
makes in a glass of water.

I was surprised at how little alarmed I felt as I sat with no
idea of what would happen, and not even a comfortable room
to return to. Margaret and I talked for almost three hours, and
our conversation seemed to me afterward to have been ex-
traordinarily sweet: witty, frivolous, daring—the kind of conversation one always hopes to have in college. It was exciting
to be outside at night, and so far aloft; the weirdly shifting
clouds above the trees and roofs made me feel that I was in a
crow's nest, looking out over unfamiliar country. Every half
hour or so, Margaret would push back her long hair, touch me
on the shoulder, and say, in a voice at once sympathetic and
sleepy, "Sarah, you have to get up early for your flight." But
neither of us really wanted to put an end to a time that it suddenly seemed we might never have again. So until the Memorial Church bell rang four o'clock, we went on sitting on the

windy balcony, swinging our legs high in the darkness, while below us, one by one, the lights went out.

# 2

Back in Philadelphia, every familiar person I met and everything around me seemed slightly skewed, a few degrees off normal. It reminded me of a science-fiction story I'd read about a planet identical to Earth, except that every proportion was subtly different—landing there drove human space travelers insane. Life at home seemed funny or tediously queer; I found myself in fits of inappropriate laughter, or filled with the impatience one feels when someone goes on and on with a boring joke. My aunt Lily, normally impeccably groomed, picked me up at the airport with her hair flattened on one side of her head, and lipstick blurred on the same side of her handsome, olive-skinned face, so that she had a Cubist look. "Sarah, you'll have to be very brave," she murmured, hugging me, and I said flippantly into the side of her perfumed neck, "I'm not the brave type."

At home Mama went around answering the doorbell and the interminably ringing telephone with a weird vivacious smile on her face; Matthew, home from law school, had the moony, famished look of a child in a UNICEF brochure. The three of us sat eating lunch without the vaguest idea of what to talk about: the web of assumptions, memories, and old associations that makes conversations within families as automatic as breathing had abruptly been ruptured for us, and we had to find new ways to behave toward one another.

After lunch we went to the hospital, which was a very modern suburban one, set like a country club on top of rolling turf hills that intersected the golf course of an actual country club next door. There in a small white room lay my father, absurdest of anyone in the family, breathing into a respirator in loud, sharp gasps that seemed affected to me, his eyebrows drawn down above his closed eyes and his cheeks puffed in a petulant, willful expression like a child having a tantrum. Mama sat and held his hand and talked into his ear, but I looked at him and wanted to shake him the way you shake a naughty child. I felt incensed at him, as if he'd played me a particularly nasty trick.

Outside the hospital windows a flock of sparrows wheeled on a whitish sky from which a few big flakes of snow were falling; to the west a development of ranch houses spread over the brown hills. I walked over to the window, stuck my hands into the back pockets of my jeans, and pressed my nose hard against the glass, thinking about times when Daddy had played jokes on me. Once when I was very little he had told me that a perfectly ordinary rosebush that he had bought at J. C. Penney was a magic flowering tree whose blossoms would form letters that would spell out my name. It had been a brief, idle tale, invented to relieve the tedium of a trip home from the shopping center, but I had dwelt on the idea all winter and spring, and in summer when the bush brought forth a perfectly ordinary constellation of roses, I had been filled with disappointment and rage.

Matthew came and stood beside me at the window, looking ridiculously young in a faded Atlantic City sweatshirt under a sports jacket. "What are we going to do?" he said, rubbing his chin with his knuckles.

"What are we going to do about what?" I said, with my nose still pressed against the window, so that a circle of water vapor grew and shrank on the glass with my breath. "Matty, have you ever heard of a kind of flowering bush that spells out letters?"

Matthew looked at me. "You know, you're being really obnoxious," he said. "You're not helping anything at all."

A nurse came up to us and told us that visiting hours for Reverend Phillips were over. I went up to the bed and laid three fingers on my father's cheek, as one does to awaken a sleeper, but the petulant expression, the childish heaving breaths did not change. Through my fingers, up my arm like an electric shock, ran the intimation of an anguish more complete than any I had ever experienced. I jerked my hand away and walked quickly out of the hospital room, pausing only to mutter to Matthew, "It's not *me* who's behaving badly!"

# 3

That night it snowed harder, a wet spring snow that threatened to break down the branches of the old azaleas around our house. At six the next morning, Mama, Matthew, and I were summoned to the hospital because Daddy had stopped breathing. The willful, childish expression had vanished from his face; within the chrome bars of the bed he looked tranquil, yet somehow more sophisticated than he had ever looked in life, with an aloof, delicately amused expression, as if his last thought had been a witticism of such subtlety that none of us could have appreciated it. And the joke was, I thought, that he wasn't there—he had slipped out of our lives as swiftly and fantastically as characters in children's stories stepped out of everyday life into Oz, or the country back of the North Wind. I leaned over the bed and rubbed my cheek against his big freckled wrist and hand that had assisted at so many christenings, weddings, baptisms, and death-beds, and felt for the first time the limited contours of a body that had often seemed to me to be larger than life.

Mama was crying, and a nurse with a turned-up nose gave her a cup of pink liquid to drink. Two doctors had been assigned to the case: Dr. Casey, who was tall, thin, and balding, with a good-humored, rather playful look on his face, and Dr. Henry, a friend of my father's, who was short, fat, and grave. Dr. Casey came into the room and said to Mama, "We're all so sorry about your husband, Mrs. Phillips. There are many of us here who followed his civil-rights work with great interest."

"His work?" said my mother in a strange, slow voice. "His work killed him." She had a faintly puzzled look in her eyes, as if she had no idea what she was saying.

"And one thing you can be glad of is that he certainly felt no pain," continued Dr. Casey smoothly. He stroked his wispy side-burns and darted at me a puzzling little wink, a wink that seemed less flirtatious than hortatory, the kind of wink a scoutmaster might dart at a charge who seemed in danger of slacking off. "There was no suffering at all."

"He left that for us," said Matthew flatly, and I stared at him. It occurred to me for the first time in my life that my mother, my brother, and I had each had a separate bond to my father, unfathomable to the others: now each of us had his own mysteri-ous store of anger and grief.

# 4

The first person who arrived when we got home from the hospi-tal was Mrs. Eakins, head of the Youth Choir and the Women's Missionary Guild at New African. Mrs. Eakins was a small, ener-getic old woman with a squashed little dark-skinned face like a

raisin—one of the avid churchwomen whom my mother sometimes described as being willing to shed any amount of Christian
blood for my father. She rang the bell and then walked into the
house before anyone came to the door. "I know it's not even
nine o'clock in the morning," she said breathlessly, "but I had
to find out how *he* is!"

"He died very early this morning," said my mother.

At those words Mrs. Eakins simply flung herself on the living-
room floor, an act that showed a resilience of muscle I never
would have dreamed she had. "Oh, my Lord, he's dead! My
pastor is dead!" she shrieked in a hoarse, guttural voice that
seemed sexless and grotesque, as if a demon were roaring from
inside her. The skirt of her dark-blue suit rucked itself up to
show a shameless piece of white nylon slip, and her feet, in black
oxfords and thick elastic stockings, beat a brief tattoo on the
carpet. The sight was both pathetic and monstrous. Matthew,
Mama, and I, our own pain eclipsed, helped her over to the sofa
and stood by numbly as the old woman continued to shriek and
writhe like a possessed person. As I watched, I reflected that she
was the first of many who would try to make my father's death
into something all their own.

# 5

In the next few days, the house seemed to fill up with old
women. There were my father's cousins from Washington, there
was my great-aunt Madeline Chavis from Binghamton, there was
the crowd of indestructible aged ladies who throughout my
childhood and adolescence had formed a murmuring background frieze for events at New African. The house overflowed
with a smell of old-fashioned cologne and pomade, and with a
continuous light, sorrowful clucking, as if the big rooms had
been invaded by a flock of elderly hens. It was impossible for me
to turn around without being hugged and kissed by some member of that aged sisterhood. Whether she was brown- or yellow-
or pink-skinned, whether she wore a wig or had thin gray hair
drawn back into a bun, she always gave me the same shrewd,
probing glance before embracing me. The old women filled the
guest bedroom with little plastic suitcases full of hairclips and
faded flannel nightgowns, and they spirited my mother away

somewhere—possibly to her bedroom, which had become a darkened sanctuary from which someone was always emerging with a cup and saucer on a tray.

Every one of the old women brought food—glorious, near-phantasmagorical food that piled up in the kitchen like a treasure from the Arabian Nights. It was the weighty southern food of my childhood holidays, but with a grandeur and ambitiousness to it that, on its own, established an occasion of high solemnity. Overflowing from the refrigerator onto the kitchen table and counters were a roast goose, a crown roast of pork, a couple of pheasants shot in Maryland by Deacon Leech, a corn pudding stuffed with oysters, glittering jars of homemade pickles and preserves, and desserts of all description, dominated by an oceanic rice pudding flavored with oranges, and a mountainous chocolate poundcake covered with rum icing and dotted with pecans. Often in the days before the funeral I found myself creeping into the kitchen at odd hours when it was unguarded by the aged fairy godmothers of our household; all alone, I would greedily, frantically taste everything, as if I were on the track of a subtle flavor that continued to elude me.

Directed by my aunts Lily and May, the old women answered the phone and the doorbell and at the same time began an inconspicuous but thorough campaign of household tasks. The crystal was washed and set out ready for use on the sideboard, linen towels were starched and placed in the bathrooms for the guests who came and went, shades all over the house were dusted and then lowered to a uniform height, so that the rooms lay in a gleaming duskiness, and the house, with its low-voiced, somberly dressed visitors, had become an entirely public place.

There was nothing at all for me to do. Mama had disappeared, and Matthew spent much of his time closeted with Uncle Freddy and a lawyer. To escape the old women, I sat upstairs in the unused maid's bathroom at the back of the house, where a trickling stream of water made rust streaks in a claw-footed bathtub, and a blue spruce scratched gloomily at the pane. I sat on the floor among stacks of old magazines and the volumes of an outdated *World Book Encyclopedia,* reading *Two Years before the Mast,* one of the books I was analyzing for my thesis. When I got tired of that, I scanned the party jokes from Matthew's old *Playboys* and looked at *National Geographic* diagrams of the sacrificial well at Chichén Itzá. One afternoon Matthew came in and found me leafing through the P volume of the *World Book.* "Look," said Matthew, dropping down on his knees beside me and grabbing the book. He opened it to a picture we'd both loved when we were little: a panorama of the Pleistocene Epoch in which everything—the rolling savannahs, the gentle hills, the curiously gnarled trees, the pelts of the big early mammals who posed in heroic attitudes around the landscape—had the same tinge of autumnal gold. "I'll be the saber-tooth," he said, his narrow, dark-lashed gaze giving me the familiar vertiginous sense of looking into my own eyes.

"I'm the woolly mammoth," I said.

It was a game we used to play with the animals in the picture: a sort of Rock, Scissors, Paper that was more interesting than it sounded because you pretended to be the animal you picked and tried to figure out ways to beat the others. We hadn't played it seriously for years, but the words to it were part of the private coded language we had shared, and the picture seemed a portrait of an epoch in our lives. It was a time, I realized, that was now as remote from Matthew and me as if a glacier had covered it. After a few seconds, my brother and I couldn't look at the *World Book* or at each other any more. I stared down at the knees of my jeans, which were white with dust, and Matthew, without saying anything else, got up and walked away.

# 6

On the night of my father's funeral, a policeman and four members of the Ushers' Guild were directing the crowd outside the church. By the time our limousine pulled up, they had begun to tell people that all the pews were filled. I had rarely been to the church at night; lit from the inside, the big Gothic building looked grander and more mysterious than it did in the daytime. The stained-glass windows shone and the bells rang out over the blocks of row houses bounded by the Delaware River and the railroad yards—neighborhoods where my parents had grown up, and which they had abandoned to raise their children outside the city.

I was dressed like an heiress: the old women who had shaken our household into the proper symbolic order had produced

from somewhere a slim black wool dress, a matching black coat
with a fur collar, sleek leather shoes, and a lace mantilla, all of
these things of an uncompromising luxurious quality that daz-
zled me a bit. Sometimes at school I had played at dressing up,
but I had never had clothes like these, nor had I ever ridden in
a limousine. When I saw how expensive and beautiful I looked,
I was filled with a surge of self-congratulatory excitement, and
with the feeling of assuming a glamorous new character with the
clothes. Once seated in the gray interior of the big black car, I
leaned my head against the window glass in an affected manner,
hoping that passers-by in the March night would see and admire
me as a tragic heroine.

As we entered the church, Mama supported by Uncle Freddy
and old Deacon Cronin, the organ was playing "Sheep May
Safely Graze." Through the music came the breathless feeling
of pressure, the vast rustling murmur of a packed crowd. There
were more people than I had ever seen at New African before,
squeezed even into the upstairs balconies that I had seen filled
only during Daddy's great Easter and Christmas ceremonies.
They stood up to see us come in, and the force of that mass
concentration on our small group caused a blush of heat over
my body, as if I were under the lens of a burning-glass. The light
in the church was dim, almost amber, giving the gilt-and-blue
ceiling, the massive oak altar, and the red-curtained baptismal
pool the look of an old-fashioned hand-colored photograph.
The rustling rows of somberly dressed people made me think of
a stand of dark grain or bamboo. When I entered, I looked
automatically for my father in the pulpit; he wasn't there, but in
an instant I saw his face down below, lying in what seemed to
be a bassinet of flowers. For a minute I felt absurdly pleased that
he should be, as usual, at the center of things at the church, but
then the sight of his face among the flowers began to puzzle and
disturb me. It was an image that I was to return to many times
in the months and years that followed, but I could never decide
what to think about it.

There were three speakers at the funeral: Dr. Shelton
Granger, a white minister who had worked with Daddy in civil-
rights election campaigns in Alabama; Father Gerald Ramsay,
an Episcopal minister and neighbor of ours, whose kind, lopsided brown face had been a familiar sight at our dinner table;
and Stuart Penn, who had grown up with Daddy at New African
and had flown in from Washington, where he headed a commis-

sion for poor people and had his name constantly in the papers. Penn had a sallow, angular face, a bit like my father's, and a forceful, blunt, magnetic way of speaking. He called my father "Jimmy," as no one else but my mother did, and at one point in his eulogy he turned suddenly in the pulpit and spoke directly to Matthew and me. "I would like to request, for Jimmy's sake, that you two kids try to do something out of the ordinary with your lives," he said, in a voice that sounded harsh and peremptory, as if he were giving an order.

I knew Penn only as one of the men in suits who had filled the living room with cigarette smoke and argument throughout my childhood; but when his bulging, rather cold brown eyes brushed across mine as I sat in the pew, I had the sensation—for the first time in many days—of connecting with my father. At the same time, I was aware of the desire to say something: a word, even a syllable, of explanation or assent. The moment came and passed almost instantaneously, and I had no idea what I might have said. Again I was aware only of the amber light, the great bank of flowers that half hid my father's face, and the massed, inquisitive gaze of the crowd on my black lace and fur. It was much the easiest to pretend to be a heroine.

# 7

The next day at about noon I went for a walk, grabbing out of an upstairs closet an old purple ski jacket that I had bought back in ninth grade. When the jacket was new, it had been puffy and stylish, with a crisp white lining printed with tiny purple pines; now it was dirty and deflated-looking, with a rip in the left arm where my mother, who wore it to hang out clothes, had caught it on a branch. In one pocket I found a wadded-up school lunch ticket with two meals still unpunched, and in the other I found an ancient stick of chewing gum, its wrapper faded to a yellowish gray. I put the gum in my mouth as I went out the door, and it immediately dissolved into a thousand tiny crumbs, each with a wisp of flavor that was like a memory of spearmint.

Outside it was gray and chilly and windless, one of the absolutely nondescript March days that nevertheless have about them a sense of secret excitement, a silent, fulminating sense of preparation for the coming change of season. Patches of dirty snow still lay on lawns and in gutters up and down the street, but the branches of the maple trees were knobby with buds. I wasn't thinking much about warm weather. To me, the stucco and fieldstone houses with their muddy lawns in the suburban noonday stillness looked inexpressibly sloppy and depressing. As I turned the corner of my street and walked toward Hopkins Place, where the houses were big and Victorian and beginning to be torn down for garden apartments, I started to have the strange idea that every house I passed was in poor repair; was, in fact, falling to pieces as I looked at it. For a very brief instant, the space of a blink, I seemed to be walking on a broad dirt road in the middle of a tremendous mutable landscape in which the main tendency seemed to be to break down, to decay. "People ought to try to keep up their property!" I thought irritably, and then realized that I had spoken aloud.

A nurse from the local hospital who was waiting at the bus stop across the street gave me a curious look, and I drew my head down into my collar. I felt suddenly that I looked genuinely eccentric in the filthy old ski jacket, my hair pulled back formally as it had been for the burial service that morning and the smeared remains of lipstick around my mouth. What I remembered most clearly about the burial was the dismal reddish color of the broken soil, and the unpleasantly smooth motion of the mechanical device that lowered the coffin into the earth; the two images seemed to have nothing to do with anything.

Talking aloud to myself, however, had suddenly recalled my father to me: he was always talking—preaching, or conferring with parties of solemn-faced men—and when he had no one else to talk to, he talked to himself, pacing in the dining room through many sleepless nights. Once when I was very small, I had crept down the back stairs and peered at him from the kitchen doorway. Wearing pajamas, he had been walking up and down, talking in a low, expressive voice and pausing occasionally to write in the notebook he kept for sermons, his face as alert and interested as if someone were walking there beside him. Remembering that, I remembered that after his funeral I had dreamed about him. In the dream he had fallen overboard from a whaling ship—like the one in *Two Years before the Mast*—and had come up from the ocean still alive but encased in a piece of iceberg. Through the ice I could see his big hands gesturing in a friendly, instructive manner while he looked straight at me and said something inaudible. It was the same word or syllable I had wanted to say in answer to Stuart Penn, and I couldn't figure out what it was.

# 8

When I took the train back up to Boston, a weird-looking kid got on at the North Philadelphia station and sat down next to me. He was fourteen or fifteen and had stringy shoulder-length hair that was a rich, almost metallic gold color, like the hair of a Madonna in a particularly garish religious picture. He had a whitish, pimply, pushed-in face and black eyes that looked almost Oriental; on his skinny body he was wearing a pair of faded orange bell-bottoms and a tight, cheap-looking leather coat, with the big cuffs and wide lapels that had just gone out of fashion. He pushed a very small knapsack with a Boy Scout emblem on it under the seat in front of him, and then he turned to me with such a bright, nutty gaze that I wondered what drug he was on. "Do you like riddles?" he asked me, without any preliminary, and my heart sank.

I was feeling numb and lightheaded, unable yet to comprehend what had happened to my life in the last week and a half. My mother had driven me to the station, and we had kissed goodbye like a couple of zombies, looking at each other with the oblique gaze of two people for whom pain had temporarily cut off communication.

"Listen, I really don't feel like talking," I said to the kid next to me, and he responded brightly, "That's OK—I'll just give the riddle, and if you don't know the answer, I'll say that, too."

He told me an elephant joke, one of the oldest in the world, and after he told it, he gave a grating high-pitched giggle. "That's a really good joke," he said. "A guy gave me a ride in this incredible customized van and told me that one. Hey—I'm on my way to Vegas. Where're you going?"

"What are you doing on the train to Boston if you're going to Las Vegas?" I asked unwillingly.

"I've got a *connection* in New York," he said, emphasizing "connection" in a spacy, mysterious way that suggested to me that he meant nothing at all by it. "Hey, listen, how old are you?"

"Twenty."

"Crazy. I'm fifteen. I got suspended from school when me and this other guy were in shop and we put a bullet in a vise and turned it until the bullet went off. It was wild, the teacher went nuts. After that I got sick of sitting around the house getting high and watching *Secret Storm* with Uncle Roman. He's my father's brother, Macedonian, just off the boat, doesn't speak a word of English—just 'yes,' 'no,' and 'TV.' Christ, what a dirtball. So I took off to go to Vegas and be a dealer or a bodyguard. Both those jobs make a lot of money. You name it, anything would be better than living in Linvilla, PA—Linvilla, armpit of Scranton, asshole of the world. Where are you going?"

"Back to school in Boston."

He went on talking in a chattering rush that convinced me that he was on speed, then suddenly, in mid-sentence, grabbed his knapsack and hopped off the train in Newark, leaving me to wonder why he had said he was going to New York. After he was gone, I realized that he had never given a ticket to the conductor.

At Penn Station in New York, a dark-haired young woman got on and sat next to me. She was a few years older than I was, dressed in jeans and an old squirrel coat; there was, however, something stately and controlled about the way she moved her shoulders and head that made her clothes seem elegant. She was carrying a paperback book, but she kept glancing at me in a lively, eager way that made me realize that I was fated, that day, to have people approach me. When we started to talk, I was struck by the contrast between the vibrant expression on her face and the strange, deliberately muted way in which she spoke. After a few minutes she told me that she was an opera student and had just won a prize in a competition in Manhattan.

"The prize I won is a scholarship to study at the Salzburg Conservatory," she said in her muted voice, regarding me with a warm, almost caressing look in her small brown eyes, as if she felt that I was partly responsible for her good fortune. "I'm walking on air, but I'm also scared out of my mind. I've been studying for years, but I never thought anything like this would happen—I mean, I was teaching *nursery* school. And my family's ecstatic—they're throwing me a big party at my aunt's house in Cranston."

Now that I knew she was a singer, I studied her strong, rather swarthy neck that rose imperiously from her red sweater; it seemed to be pulsing with life and health.

"You'll be famous," I said, feeling a little jealous.

"That part doesn't even count to me," she said, though her expression made me suspect that it did. "What matters is that something—at last—has happened to me!"

She got off at New Haven, first giving me her name—Lucy Consalves—and I settled back to stare out at the wintry beaches passing by the train windows as we continued through Connecticut. It was about three-thirty in the afternoon. The sky over the water was a striated gray, and the sea was a deeper gray, with the foam of the waves a startling, recurring flicker of yellowish white that seemed like a repetitive signal of nearly human expression—the wink of an eye or the waving of a handkerchief. A kid of about seventeen or eighteen was jogging on the sand; he was black, and I wondered briefly what on earth he was doing on a Connecticut beach. The lowering light gave the broad expanse of sea and marsh and sky around him a curiously contained, interior feeling. A few gulls skimmed the waves, and I thought of the New African Baptist Church, where the stuffed white dove representing the Holy Spirit still hung on a string over the baptismal pool, and where the people had stood crowded as close as marsh grass to witness my father's last appearance.

The train moved past the seascape and the jogger, on toward Rhode Island, and I closed my eyes. Exhausted as I was, I had a brief new impression: that the world was a place full of kids in transit, people like the jogger and Lucy Consalves and that punk from Linvilla, PA, all of them, inexplicably, bound on excursions that might end up being glorious or stupid or violent, but that certainly moved in a direction away from anything they had ever known. I was one of them, and although I didn't know what direction I was heading in, and had only a faint idea yet of what I was leaving behind, the sense of being in motion was a thrill that made up for a lot. I sat and squeezed my eyes tighter and hoped that it would turn out to be enough for me.

ANDREA LEE was born in Philadelphia and received her bachelor's and master's degrees from Harvard University. Her first book, *Russian Journal*, was nominated for a National Book Award and received the 1984 Jean Stein Award from the American Academy and Institute of Arts and Letters. *Sarah Phillips* is her first novel. Miss Lee is a staff writer for *The New Yorker*. She and her husband live in Rome.